IN PRAISE OF MUSIC

AN ANTHOLOGY

EDITED BY

RICHARD LEWIS

In Praise of Music

THE ORION PRESS

NEW YORK

The Editor has made every effort to trace the ownership of all copyrighted material. In the event of any question arising as to the use of any selections the Editor, while expressing regret for any error he may have made, will be pleased to make the necessary correction in future editions of this book. Thanks are due to the following authors, publishers, publications and representatives for permission to use the selections indicated:

The selections by Confucius are from *The Wisdom of Confucius* edited by Lin Yutang. Copyright, 1938, by Random House, Inc. The selections by Plato are from *The Dialogues of Plato* translated by B. Jowett. Copyright, 1920, by Oxford University Press. The selection by Aristotle is from *The Basic Works of Aristotle* edited by Richard McKeon. Copyright, 1941, by Random House, Inc. The selection by Mr. Tut-Tut is from *The Wisdom of China and India* edited by Lin Yutang. Copyright, 1942, by Random House, Inc. The selection by Baudelaire is from *Intimate Journals* translated by Christopher Isherwood. Copyright, 1947, Marcel Rodd. The selection by Henri Bergson is from *Time and Free Will* translated by F. L. Pogson. Copyright, 1910, The Macmillan Co. and George Allen and Unwin, Ltd. The selection by Romain Rolland is from *Jean Christophe* translated by Gilbert Cannan. Copyright, 1910, by Henry Holt & Co., and William Heinemann, Ltd. The selection by James Gibbons Huneker is from *Mezzotints in Modern Music*. Copyright, Charles Scribner's Sons. The selection by W. J. Turner is from *Orpheus, Or the Music of the Future*. By permission of E. P. Dutton & Co., Inc. and Rutledge & Kegan Paul, Ltd. The selection by Remy de Gourmont is from *The Translations of Ezra Pound*. All rights reserved. Reprinted by permission of New Directions, Publishers. The selections by George Santayana are from *The Life of Reason*. By permission of Charles Scribner's Sons and Constable & Co., Ltd. The selection by Wassily Kandinsky is from *Concerning the Spiritual in Art*. Courtesy of George Wittenborn, Inc. The Documents of Modern Art, Vol. 5. The selection by Jacques Maritain is from *Creative Intuition in Art and Poetry*. By permission of the Bollingen Foundation, New York. The selection by Susanne Langer is from *Feeling and Form*. Permission of Charles Scribner's Sons and Rutledge and Kegan Paul, Ltd. The selection by Sacheverell Sitwell is from *Splendours and Miseries*. By permission of the author. The selection by Lin Yutang is from *The Importance of Living*. Copyright, 1937, by The John Day Co., Inc. The selection by Aldous Huxley is from *Music at Night* by Aldous Huxley. Reprinted by permission of Harper and Row, Publishers. The selection by David Mannes is from *Music is My Faith*. The selection from the Shiva Pradosha Stotra is from *The Dance of Shiva* by Ananda K. Coomarswami. By permission of Farrar, Straus & Cudahy, Inc. The selection from *Tales of the Hasidim, The Early Masters* is by Martin Buber. Copyright, 1947, by Schocken Books, Inc., New York. The selections by Gerard M. Hopkins are from *A Hopkins Reader* edited by John Pick. By permission of Oxford University Press. The selection and the poem, "Music" by Wilfred Owen are from *The Poems of Wilfred Owen*. All rights reserved. Printed by permission of New Directions, Publishers and Chatto and Windus, Ltd. The selection by Bernard Berenson is from *Rumor and Reflection*. Copyright, 1952, by Bernard Berenson. Reprinted by permission of Simon and Schuster, Inc. and John Constable, Ltd. The selection by George Bernard Shaw is from *Preface to London Music in 1888-89 As Heard by Corno di Bassetto*. By permission of the Public Trustee and The Society of Authors,

New Directions, Publishers. The selection by Stephen Spender is from *The Making of a Poem*. Reprinted by permission of the Partisan Review and the author. The poem "The Composer" by W. H. Auden is from *The Collected Poetry of W. H. Auden*. Random House and Faber and Faber, Ltd. The poem "Musician" by Louise Bogan is from *The Collected Poems of Louise Bogan*. Farrar, Straus & Cudahy, Inc. The poem by Wallace Stevens is from *The Collected Poems of Wallace Stevens*. Alfred A. Knopf, Inc. The poem "Music" by Walter de la Mare is reprinted by permission of The Literary Trustees of Walter de la Mare and The Society of Authors as their representative. The selection by Lin Yutang is from *The Importance of Living*. Copyright William Heinemann, Ltd. The selection by Edith Sitwell is from *Time Magazine*, Jan. 17, 1955.

The editor would like to take this opportunity to sincerely thank Miss Robin Fox, for her excellent preliminary designs; Miss Georgette Schnir, for her careful typing of the manuscript; Mr. Julius Weber, for his kind help in photographing illustrations; Mr. William Cole, for his valuable advice; Mr. Philip Grausman, for his unfailing friendship and critical insights; Miss Frances Menk, for her patience and aid during the final stages; Miss Julie Colmore, for her encouragements and suggestions; and Mr. Howard Greenfeld, for his thorough editorial guidance, and gratifying enthusiasm and understanding throughout the preparation of this book.

TO MY PARENTS WITH LOVE

Contents

II THE PERSONAL NOTE

XII

In Praise of Music

XIII

Contents

xv

Contents

Introduction

We are surrounded by such a mélange of melodies and rhythms, persistently weaving their spells into the fabric of our lives, that it is now possible to feel that for all its glories, music can and does become something of an intrusion. Very often this intrusion is created by a fellow human being who plays an endless variety of musical pleasures at the loudest possible volume. Sometimes it is the agonized decision that one must make in order to pick the choicest musical plum from the over-grown, over-populated arbor of musical pleasures. Whatever this intrusion may be, we find ourselves showered with music, causing a condition in which we are taking music for granted. Just as the love between two people wanes when it is taken for granted, so too with an art as bountiful and pleasure-giving as music. Its very accessibility has brought it so near to us that we have often neglected to give it its honored place. Because we are sometimes in a state of listening without always hearing, soothed rather than uplifted, agreeably scintillated rather than profoundly moved, music has lost some of its power as a deity in the world of art. The astonishing phenomenon that music can exist at all, that so much that is beautiful has been created within its domain and that a large percentage of our mortal joy can be realized

Introduction

through and by music—the fact that the very awareness of these thoughts is often absent from our thinking is a cause of concern and distress.

If this book can serve a purpose it is hoped that it will reveal a few of the many ways in which music is an experience that touches many lives, giving, as it moves from listener to listener, an unparalleled richness of satisfaction. Now, more than ever, as the sound of music reaches an ever-growing audience we should remember the distinctive qualities of this great art and feel, as Nietzsche did, that "Without music, life would be a mistake." We must, after having spoken all the words of praise, give to music its only demand, and in the end, its highest praise—we must begin to listen.

Richard Lewis
October 6th, 1962

I

Thoughts, Maxims and
Speculations

The joy of the heart begets song.

The Talmud

There is a temple in heaven that is opened only through song.

The Talmud

Virtue is our favorite flower. Music is the perfume of that flower.

Le Ly-Kim A Ritual 7th Century B.C.

When you see the type of a nation's dance, you know its character. . . .
    Man is gifted with blood and breath and a conscious mind, but his feel-
ing of sorrow and happiness and joy and anger depend on circumstances.

4
In Praise of Music

His definite desires arise from reactions toward the material world. Therefore, when a somber and depressing type of music prevails, we know the people are distressed and sorrowful. When a languorous, easy type of music with many long-drawn-out airs prevails, we know that the people are peaceful and happy. When a strong and forceful type of music prevails, beginning and ending with a full display of sounds, we know that the people are hearty and strong. When a pure, pious and majestic type of music prevails, we know that the people are pious. When a gentle, lucid and quietly progressing type of music prevails, we know that the people are kind and affectionate. When lewd, exciting and upsetting music prevails, we know that the people are immoral. . . .

When the soil is poor, things do not grow, and when fishing is not regulated according to the seasons, then fishes and turtles do not mature; when the climate deteriorates, animal and plant life degenerates, and when the world is chaotic, the rituals and music become licentious. We find then a type of music that is rueful without restraint and joyous without calm. . . .

Therefore, the superior man tries to create harmony in the human heart by a rediscovery of human nature, and tries to promote music as a means to the perfection of human culture. When such music prevails and the people's minds are led toward the right ideals and aspirations, we may see the appearance of a great nation.

Character is the backbone of our human culture, and music is the flowering of character. The metal, stone, string and bamboo instruments are the instruments of music. The poem gives expression to our heart, the song gives expression to our voice, and the dance gives expression to our movements. These three arts take their rise from the human soul, and then are given further expression by means of the musical instruments. Therefore, from the depth of sentiment comes the clarity of form and from the strength of the mood comes the spirituality of its atmosphere. This harmony of spirit springs forth from the soul and finds expression or blossoms forth in the form of music. Therefore, music is the one thing in which there is no use trying to deceive others or make false pretenses. . . .

Confucius (c. 551-479 B.C.) On Music

Music rises from the human heart. When the emotions are touched, they are expressed in sounds, and when the sounds take definite forms, we have music. Therefore the music of a peaceful and prosperous country is quiet and joyous, and the government is orderly; the music of a country in turmoil shows dissatisfaction and anger, and the government is chaotic; and the music of a destroyed country shows sorrow and remembrance of the past and the people are distressed. Thus we see music and government are directly connected with one another.

Confucius (c. 551-479 B.C.) On Music

If the king loves music it is well with the land.

Mencius (fl. 3rd century) Discourses

A lover of music like yourself ought surely to have heard the story of the grasshoppers, who are said to have been human beings in an age before the Muses. And when the Muses came and song appeared they were ravished with delight; and singing always, never thought of eating and drinking, until at last in their forgetfulness they died. And now they live again in the grasshoppers; and this is the return which the Muses make to them—they neither hunger, nor thirst, but from the hour of their birth are always singing, and never eating or drinking; and when they die they go and inform the Muses in heaven who honours them on earth. They win the love of Terpsichore for the dancers by their report of them; of Erato for the lovers, and of the other Muses for those who do them honour, according to the several ways of honouring them;—of Calliope the eldest Muse and of Urania who is next to her, for the philosophers, of whose music the grasshoppers make report to them; for these are the Muses who are chiefly concerned with heaven and thought, divine as well as human, and they have the sweetest utterance.

Plato (427?-347 B.C.) Phaedrus

9
Thoughts, Maxims and Speculations

Now the most hostile are the most opposite, such as hot and cold, bitter and sweet, moist and dry, and the like. And my ancestor, Asclepius, knowing how to implant friendship and accord in these elements, was the creator of our art, as our friends the poets here tell us, and I believe them; and not only medicine in every branch, but the arts of gymnastic and husbandry are under his dominion. Any one who pays the least attention to the subject will also perceive that in music there is the same reconcilation of opposites; and I suppose that this must have been the meaning of Heracleitus, although his words are not accurate; for he says that The One is united by disunion, like the harmony of the bow and the lyre. Now there is an absurdity in saying that harmony is discord or is composed of elements which are still in a state of discord. But what he probably meant was, that harmony is composed of differing notes of higher or lower pitch which disagreed once, but are now reconciled by the art of music; for if the higher and lower notes still disagreed, there could be no harmony,—clearly not. For harmony is a symphony, and a symphony is an agreement; but an agreement of disagreements while they disagree there cannot be; you cannot harmonize that which disagrees. In like manner rhythm is compounded of elements short and long, once differing and now in accord; which accordance, as in the former instance, medicine, so in all these other cases, music implantes, making love and unison to grow up among them; and thus music, too, is concerned with the principles of love in their application to harmony and rhythm.

Plato (427?-347 B.C.) Symposium

But music is pursued, not only as an alleviation of past toil, but also providing recreation. And who can say whether, having this use, it may not also have a nobler one? In addition to this common pleasure, felt and shared in by all (for the pleasure given by music is natural, and therefore adapted to all ages and characters), may it not have also some influence over the character and the soul? It must have such an influence if characters are affected by it. And that they are so affected is proved in many ways, and not least by the power which the songs of Olympus exercise; for beyond question they inspire enthusiasm and enthusiasm is an emotion of the ethical part of the soul. Besides, when men hear imitations, even apart from the rhythms and tunes themselves, their feelings move in sympathy. Since then music is a pleasure, and virtue consists in rejoicing and loving and hating aright, there is clearly nothing which we are so much concerned to acquire and to cultivate as the power of forming right judgments, and of taking delight in good dispositions and noble actions. Rhythm and melody supply imitations of anger and gentleness, and also of courage and temperance, and of all the qualities contrary to these, and of the other qualities of character, which hardly fall short of the actual affections, as we know from our own experience, for in listening to such strains our souls undergo a change.

Aristotle (384-322 B.C.) Politics

Song, mortals' sweetest pleasure.

Musaeus (500 A.D.)

Nothing exists without music; for the universe itself is said to have been framed by a kind of harmony of sounds, and the heaven itself revolves under the tones of that harmony.

Isidore of Seville (c. 570-636) Eytomologies

Musicke doth withdraw our mindes from earthly cogitations, lifteth up our spirits into heaven, maketh them light and celestial.

St. John Chrysostom (345-407)

When God saw that many men were lazy, and gave themselves only with difficulty to spiritual reading, He wished to make it easy for them, and added the melody to the Prophet's words, that all being rejoiced by the charm of the music, should sing to Him with gladness.

St. John Chrysostom (345-407)

Who is he bearing the sense of a man which is not ashamed to ende the day without the singing of Psalms, seeing even the little birds with solemne devotion and sweet notes do both begin and end the daie.

St. Ambrose (340-397) Praise of Musicke

Song awakens the soul to a glowing longing for what the song contains; song soothes the lusts of the flesh; it banishes wicked thoughts, aroused by invisible foes; it acts like dew to the soul, making it fertile for accomplishing good acts; it makes the pious warrior noble and strong in suffering terrible pain; it is a healing ointment for the wounds suffered in the battle of life; St. Paul calls song the 'sword of the spirit' because it protects the pious knight against the invisible enemy; for 'the Word of God' if sung in emotion has the power to expel demons. All this gives the soul the force to acquire the virtues of devotion and is brought to the pious by ecclesiastic songs.

Anonymous (c. 370 A.D.) "Questions and Answers to the Believers"

Pliny says that there is a certain land in which neither dew nor rain falls. Consequently, there is a general aridness; but in this country there is a single fountain, from which, when people would draw water, they are accustomed to approach with all kinds of musical instruments, and so march around it for a length of time.

The melody which they thus produce causes the water to rise to the mouth of the spring, and makes it flow forth in great abundance, so that all men are able to obtain as much as they will.

Gesta Romanorum (14th century)

To some people music is like *food;* to others like *medicine;* to others like a *fan.*

Arabian Nights

Gladden thine heart, drum thine drum, and pipe thine pipe.

Arabian Nights

13
Thoughts, Maxims and
Speculations

14
In Praise of Music

Nothing on earth is so well suited to make the sad merry, the merry sad, to give courage to the despairing, to make the proud humble, to lessen envy and hate, as music.

Martin Luther (1483-1546)

15
Thoughts, Maxims and Speculations

Music is one of the greatest gifts that God has given us: it is divine and therefore Satan is its enemy. For with its aid many dire temptations are overcome; the devil does not stay where music is.

Martin Luther (1483-1546) Table Talk and Letters

. . . Whosoever is harmonically composed delights in harmony; which makes me much distrust the symmetry of those heads which declaim against all Church-Musick. For my self, not only from my obedience, but my particular Genius, I do embrace it: for even that vulgar and Tavern-Musick, which makes one man merry, another mad, strikes in me a deep fit of devotion, and a profound contemplation of the First Composer. There is something in it of Divinity more than the ear discovers: it is an Hiero-glyphical and shadowed lesson of the whole World, and creatures of God; I will not say, with Plato, the soul is an harmony, but harmonical, and hath its nearest sympathy unto Musick: thus some, whose temper of body agrees, and humours the constitution of their souls, are born Poets, though indeed all are naturally inclined unto Rhythme. . .

Sir Thomas Browne (1605-1682) Religio Medici

Skarlet is no color to him that sees it not, an Emeraul not precious to him that knowes it not. But Musicke, God bee thanked, is no nightbird, she hath flown through the whole world in the ope face and sight of al me.

And ye sun hath not had a larger theater wherin to display his beams, the musick to lay ope her sweetness. Look into al ages, she hath grown up with them. Look into al places, she hath enfranchised herself within them; look into al estates, shee hath no sooner come, but welcome unto them. Antiquitie which nowe adayes everie greene head will needes set to schoole, and make subiect to the overlashing pregnancy of his yong wit, derives her even from Saturnes time, when the world was skant sheld.

John Case (?-1600) The Praise of Musicke

Many and sundry are the means which philosophers and physicians have prescribed to exhilarate a sorrowful heart, to divert those fixed and intent cares and meditations, which in this malady so much offend; but in my judgement none so present, none so powerful, none so apposite as a cup of strong drink, mirth, music, and merry company. . . . . *Musica est mentis*

medicina maestae, (music is) a roaring-meg against melancholy, to rear and revive the languishing soul; "affecting not only the ears, but the very arteries, the vital and animal spirits, it erects the mind, and makes it nimble" (Lemnius, *Instit. cap.* 44). This it will effect in the most dull, severe, and sorrowful souls," expel grief with mirth, and if there be any clouds, dust, or dregs of cares yet lurking in our thoughts, most powerfully it wipes them all away" (Sarisbur. *Polycrat.* lib. 1, *cap.* 6), and that which is more, it will perform all this in an instant: cheer up the countenance, expel austerity, bring in hilarity" (Girald. Gamb. *cap.* 12 *Topog.* Hiber.), "inform our manners, mitigate anger." Athenaeus (*Deipnosophist. lib.* 14, *cap.* 10) calleth it an infinite treasure to such as are endowed with it. . . . . Many other properties Cassiodorus, *epist.* 4, reckons up of this our divine music, not only to expel the greatest griefs, but "it doth extenuate fears and furies, appeaseth cruelty, abateth heaviness, and to such as are watchful it causeth quiet rest; it takes away spleen and hatred," be it instrumental, vocal, with strings, wind, *quoe a spiritu, sine manuum dexteritate gubernetur* (such as are played with the breath, without any action of the hands), etc.; it cures all irksomeness and heaviness of the soul. Labouring men that sing to their work can tell as much, and so can soldiers when they go to fight, whom

terror of death cannot so much affright as the sound of trumpet, drum, fife, and such-like music animates; *metus enim mortis*, as Censorinus informeth us, *musica depellitur* (for the fear of death can be banished by music). "It makes a child quiet," the nurse's song; and many times the sound of a trumpet on a sudden, bells ringing, a carman's whistle, a boy singing some ballad tune early in the street, alters, revives, recreates a restless patient that cannot sleep in the night, etc. In a word, it is so powerful a thing that it ravisheth the soul, *regina sensuum*, the queen of the senses, by sweet pleasure (which is a happy cure), and corporal tunes pacify our incorporeal soul; *sine ore loquens, dominatum in animam exercet* (speaking without a mouth, it exercises domination over the soul), and carries it beyond itself, helps, elevates, extends it. Scaliger, *exercit.* 302, gives a reason of these effects," because the spirits about the heart take in that trembling and dancing air into the body, are moved together, and stirred up with it," or else the mind, as some suppose, harmonically composed, is roused up at the tunes of music. And 'tis not only men that are so affected, but almost all other creatures. You know the tale of Hercules, Gallus, Orpheus, and Amphion, *felices animas* (blessed souls) Ovid calls them, that could *saxa*

other animals, dance after their pipes: the dog and hare, wolf and lamb; *movere sono testudinis* etc. make stocks and stones, as well as beasts and *vicinumque lupo proebuit agna latus* (the lamb lay down by the side of the wolf); *clamosus graculus, stridula cornix, et Jovis aquila* (the chattering daw, the croaking rook, the eagle of Jove), as Philostratus describes it in his Images, stood all gaping upon Orpheus; and trees pulled up by the roots came to hear him, *Et comitem quercum pinus amica trahit* (the pine brought the oak in company).

Arion made fishes follow him, which, as common experience evinceth, are much affected with music. All singing-birds are much pleased with it, especially nightingales, if we may believe Calcagninus; and bees amongst the rest, though they be flying away, when they hear any tingling sound, will tarry behind. "Harts, hinds, horses, dogs, bears, are exceedingly delighted with it" (Scal. *exerc.* 302); elephants, Agrippa adds, *lib.* 2, *cap.* 24; and in Lydia in the midst of a lake there be certain floating islands (if ye will believe it), that after music will dance.

Robert Burton (1577-1640) The Anatomy of Melancholy

Generally, music feedeth the disposition of spirit which it findeth.

Francis Bacon (1561-1626) Sylva Sylvarum

But to the purpose: this variable composition of man's body hath made it as an Instrument easy to distemper; and therefore the Poets did well to conjoin Music and Medicine in Apollo; because the Office of Medicine is but to tune this curious harp of man's body and to reduce it to Harmony.

Francis Bacon (1561-1626) Advancement of Learning

20
In Praise of Music

When Musik shall teach nothing but honest for delite, and pleasant for note, comile for the place, and semelie for the person, suitable to the thing and servicable to circumstance, can that humor corrupt, which bredeth such delite. . . ?

Richard Mulcaster (1530?-1611) The Elementarie

21
Thoughts, Maxims and Speculations

During a drizzling rain, open a volume leisurely; against the breeze, play the string instrument alone.

Mr. Tut-Tut (17th century) Proverbs

When the rain is over and the air is cool, when your affairs are few and your mind is at ease, you listen to the lingering notes of some neighbor's flute chasing after the clear clouds and the receding rain, and every note seems to drop and sink into your soul.

Mr. Tut-Tut (17th century) Proverbs

Music is good to the melancholy, bad to those who mourn, and neither good nor bad to the deaf.

Benedict de Spinoza (1632-1677)

Women and music should never be dated.

Oliver Goldsmith (1728-1744) She Stoops to Conquer

Music is a calculation which the soul makes unconsciously in secret.

Gottfried Wilhelm von Leibnitz (1646-1716) The Monadology

Without music the state cannot exist. All the disorders, all the wars we behold throughout the world occur only because of the neglect to learn music. Does not war result from lack of unison among men? Thus, were all men to learn music, would not this be the means of agreement between them and of seeing universal peace reign all over the world?

Molière (1622-1673) Le Bourgeois Gentilhomme

Music, the greatest good that mortals know.
And all of heaven we have below.

Joseph Addison (1672-1719) Song for St. Cecilia's Day

Music is the most sensuous of arts to loving souls.

Honoré de Balzac (1799-1850) The Hated Son

In painting his Saint-Cecilia, Raphael gave the preference to music over poetry. And he was right; music appeals to the heart, whereas writing is addressed to the intellect; it communicates ideas directly, like perfume.

Honoré de Balzac (1799-1850) Massimilla Doni

Modern music, a language a thousand times richer than the language of words, is to speech what thought is to its utterance; it arouses sensations and ideas in their primitive form, in that part of us where sensations and ideas have their birth, but leaves them as they are in each of us. That power over our inmost being is one of the grandest facts in music.

Honoré de Balzac (1799-1850) Massimilla Doni

For I consider music as a very innocent diversion, and perfectly compatible with the profession of a clergyman.

Jane Austen (1775-1817) Pride and Prejudice

Music revives the recollections it would appease.

Mme. de Staël (1766-1817)

... what is music without a touch of pensive sadness in it?

Stendhal (1783-1842) Life of Rossini

Pure music, quite apart from all other conceptions of the imagination touches the nerves and all organs of hearing and thus changes our inner feelings. . . . The entire being begins to resound. . . . Our feeling is nothing but an inner music, a constant oscillation of the vital nerves. Everything that surrounds us, all our new ideas and sensations increase or diminish, strengthen or weaken the state of these inner oscillations. Music touches the nerves in a peculiar manner and results in a singular playfulness, a quite special communication that cannot be described in words. Music represents the inner feeling in the exterior air, and expresses what precedes, accompanies, or follows all verbal utterance.

Wilhelm Heinse (1749-1803) Ardinghello

In truth, there is nothing like music to fill the moment with substance, whether it attune the quiet mind to reverence and worship, or whether it make the mobile senses dance in exultation. . . . .

Johann Wolfgang von Goethe (1749-1832) Letter to Zelter, Oct. 19, 1829

In music the dignity of art seems to find supreme expression. There is no subject matter to be discounted. It is all form and significant content. It elevates and ennobles whatever it expresses.

Johann Wolfgang von Goethe (1749-1832) Maxims and Reflections

The music of modern composers, too, seems to emphasize sensuality to an excessive degree and thereby flatters the current taste, which wants to be

25
Thoughts, Maxims and
Speculations

pleasantly titillated, and hates being deeply gripped, vigorously stirred or elevated to higher spheres. . . .

Friedrich Schiller (1759-1805)

So is music an asylum. It takes us out of the actual and whispers to us dim secrets that startle our wonder as to who we are, and for what, whence and whereto. All the great interrogatories, like questioning angels, float in on its waves of sound.

Ralph Waldo Emerson (1803-1882) Journals 1836-38

O! Music, echo of another world, manifestation of a divine being within ourselves, when speech is impotent and our hearts are numb, yours alone is the voice with which men cry out to one another from the depths of their prison, you it is who end their desolation, in whom are resolved the lonely outpourings of their grief.

Jean-Paul (1763-1825)

No more than any other talent is that for music susceptible of complete enjoyment where there is no second party to appreciate its exercise.

Edgar Allan Poe (1809-1849)

The unutterable depth of all music by virtue of which it floats through our consciousness as the vision of a paradise firmly believed in yet ever distant from us, and by which also it is so fully understood and yet so inexplicable, rests on the fact that it restores to us all the emotions of our inmost nature, but entirely without reality and far removed from their pain.

Arthur Schopenhauer (1788-1860) The World as Will and Idea

Music excavates Heaven.

Charles Baudelaire (1821-1867) Intimate Journals

Music is the vapor of art. It is to poetry what reverie is to thought, what fluid is to liquid, what the ocean of clouds is to the ocean of waves.

Victor Hugo (1802-1885) Les Rayons et les Ombres

In a sense, any predicable is true of music: just as one may say anything of God, because, being Infinite, there is nothing He is not.

Sidney Lanier (1842-1881) On Music

Music is love in search of a word.

Sidney Lanier (1842-1881) The Symphony

30

In Praise of Music

All art constantly aspires towards the condition of music. For while in all other works of art it is possible to distinguish the matter from the form, and the understanding can always make this distinction, yet is the constant effort of art to obliterate it. That the mere matter of a poem, for instance, its subject, its given incidents or situation; that the mere matter of a picture —the actual circumstances of an event, the actual topography of a land-scape—should be nothing without the form, the spirit of the handling; that this form, this mode of handling, should become an end in itself, should penetrate every part of the matter:—this is what all art constantly strives after, and achieves in different degrees. . . .

It is the art of music which most completely realises this artistic ideal, this perfect identification of form and matter. In its ideal, consummate moments, the end is not distinct from the means, the form from matter, the subject from the expression; they inhere in and completely saturate each other; and to it, therefore, to the condition of its perfect moments, all the arts may be supposed constantly to tend and aspire. Music, then, and not poetry, as is so often supposed, is the true type, or measure of perfected art. Therefore although each art has its incommunicable element, its un-translatable order of impressions, its unique mode of reaching the 'imaginative reason,' yet the arts may be represented as continually struggling after the law or principle of music, to a condition which music alone completely realises; and one of the chief functions of aesthetic criticism, dealing with the products of art, new or old, is to estimate the degree in which each of those products approaches, in this sense, to musical law. . . .

Walter Pater (1839-1894) The Renaissance

In song and dance man expresses himself as a member of a higher community; he has forgotten how to walk and speak; he is about to take a dancing flight into the air. His very gestures bespeak enchantment. Just as the animals now talk, just as the earth yields milk and honey, so from him emanate supernatural sounds. He feels himself a god, he himself now walks about enchanted, in ecstasy, like to the gods whom he saw walking about in his dreams.

Friedrich Nietzsche (1844-1900) The Birth of Tragedy

Without music life would be a mistake.

Friedrich Nietzsche (1844-1900) Twilight of the Idols

Thus, in music, the rhythm and measure suspend the normal flow of our sensations and ideas by causing our attention to swing to and fro between fixed points, and they take hold of us with such force that even the faintest imitation of a groan will suffice to fill us with the utmost sadness. If musical sounds affect us more powerfully than the sounds of nature, the reason is that nature confines itself to *expressing* feelings, whereas music *suggests* them to us.

Henri Bergson (1859-1941) Time and Free Will

Everything is music for the born musician. Everything that throbs, or moves, or stirs, or palpitates—sunlit summer days, nights when the wind howls, flickering light, the twinkling of the stars, storms, the song of birds, the buzzing of insects, the murmuring of trees, voices, loved or loathed, familiar fireside sounds, a creaking door, blood moving in the veins in the silence of the night—everything that is is music; all that is needed is that it should be heard.

Romain Rolland (1866-1944) Jean-Christophe

32
In Praise of Music

The love of music seems to exist for its own sake.

Herbert Spencer (1820-1903) Essays on Education

33
Thoughts, Maxims and Speculations

It is not always meet and just that we exhibit to the gaze of an incurious world our intellectual Lares and Penates. There is something almost indecent in the way we rend our mental privacies, our heart sanctuaries. To the artist in prose, the temptation to be utterly subjective is chilled by the thought of the sacrifice. Hamlet-like, he may feel that wearing his heart on his sleeve will never compensate him for the holiness of solitude, no matter if the heart he dissects be of unusual color and splendor. Far happier is the tone poet. Addressing a selected audience, appealing to sensibilities firm and tastes exquisitely cultured, he may still remain secluded. His musical phrases are cryptic and even those who run fastest may not always read. The veil that hangs hazily about all great art works is the Tanit veil that obscures the holy of holies from the gaze of the rude, the blasphemous. The golden reticence of the music artist saves him from the mortifying misunderstandings of the worker in verse, and spares him the pang which must come from the nudity of the written word.

James Gibbons Huneker (1860-1921) Mezzotints in Modern Music

Music is the imagination of love in *sound*. It is what man imagines of his life, and his life is love.

W. J. Turner (1889-   ) Orpheus, or The Music of the Future

What is most admirable in music is the hearing and soul of men.

Remy de Gourmont (1858-1915) Poudre aux Moineaux

It (music) makes the dumb speak, and plucks from the animal heart potentialities of expression which might render it, perhaps, even more than human.

George Santayana (1863-1952) Reason in Art

Music is like those branches which some trees put forth close to the ground, far below the point where the other boughs separate; almost a tree by itself, it has nothing but the root in common with its parent. Somewhat in this fashion music diverts into an abstract sphere a part of those forces which abound beneath the point at which human understanding grows articulate. It flourishes on saps which other branches of ideation are too narrow or rigid to take up. These elementary substances the musician can spiritualise by his special methods, taking away their reproach and redeeming them from blind intensity.

George Santayana (1863-1952) Reason in Art

A painter, who finds no satisfaction in mere representation, however artistic, in his longing to express his internal life, cannot but envy the ease with which music, the least material of the arts today, achieves this end. And from this results that modern desire for rhythm in painting, for mathematical, abstract construction, for repeated notes of color, for setting color in motion, and so on.

Wassily Kandinsky (1866-1944) Concerning the Spiritual in Art

Music comes eons before religion. . . .

Alfred North Whitehead (1861-1947)

Then there is in the soul of the poet an enlarged musical stir, a music no longer almost imperceptible, but more and more cogent, in which the soundless rhythmic and harmonic relations between intuitive pulsions, together with their soundless melody, emerge into consciousness. This enlarged musical stir is the spontaneous start of operative exercise; with it the process of expression begins, in a first transient and tendential stage. Yet this music is still an inaudible music—not the music of the words, but the music of the intuitive pulsions within the soul.

Jacques Maritain (1882-   ) Creative Intuition in Art and Poetry

The real basis of music appreciation is the same as of music making: the recognition of forms in virtual time, charged with the vital import of all art, the ways of human feeling. It is the perception of feeling through a purely apparent flow of life existing only in time. Anything the listener does or thinks of to make this experience more telling is musically good. This is not to say, however, that anything people like to do during music is good, since they often confuse "enjoying music" with enjoying themselves unmusically during music. But anything that helps concentration and sustains the illusion—be it inward singing, following a half-comprehended score, or dreaming in dramatic images—may be one's personal way to understanding. For *listening* is the primary musical activity. The musician listens to his own idea before he plays, before he writes. The basis of all musical advance is more comprehensive hearing. And the one support that every artist must have if he is to go on creating music is a world that listens.

Susanne K. Langer (1895-   ) The Musical Matrix

There has been demonstration of the universal truth by fugue, and it may be that more wisdom is to be found in that than in the religions and religious books of all the world together.

Sacheverell Sitwell (1879-   ) Orpheus and His Lyre

Music is pure sentiment itself, dispensing entirely with the language of words with which alone the intellect can operate. Music can portray for us the sounds of cowbells and fishmarkets and the battlefield; it can portray for us even the delicacy of flowers, the undulating motion of the waves, or the sweet serenity of the moonlight; but the moment it steps outside the limit of the senses and tries to portray for us a philosophic idea, it must be considered decadent and the product of a decadent world.

Lin Yutang (1895-   ) The Importance of Living

What is true of painting is equally true of music. Music "says" things about the world, but in specifically musical terms. Any attempt to reproduce these musical statements "in our own words" is necessarily doomed

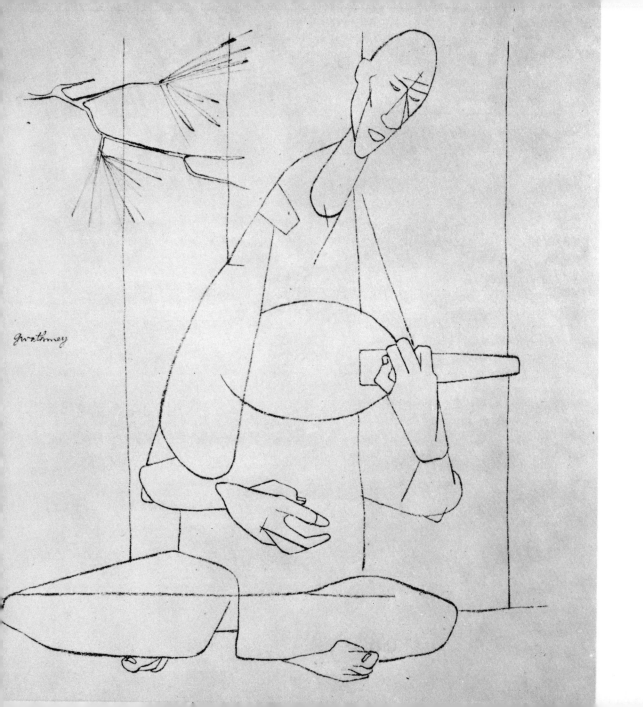

to failure. We cannot isolate the truth contained in a piece of music; for it is a beauty-truth and inseparable from its partner. The best we can do is to indicate in the most general terms the nature of the musical beauty-truth under consideration and to refer curious truth-seekers to the original.

Aldous Huxley (1894-   ) Music at Night

39
Thoughts, Maxims and Speculations

Above all—at least to me—music is the perfect universal language. This is a platitude only because it happens like other platitudes to be based on incontrovertible truth. The only times when I have witnessed a state approaching the brotherhood of man have been moments of music, when hundreds of hearts beat to the same rhythm and lifted to the same phrase and when all hate, all envy, all greed were washed away by the nobility of sound. Words are so often the agents of destruction; music—good music —can only build. And to learn the language of music—or at least to respond to it—one needs only an ear and a heart. It is only the deaf or the spiritually atrophied who do not somehow feel themselves exalted and purified in the presence of great music.

David Mannes (1866-1959) Music is My Faith

II

The Personal Note

Now the spirit of the Lord had departed from Saul, and an evil spirit from the Lord terrified him. And Saul's servants said unto him: 'Behold now, an evil spirit from God terrifieth thee. Let our Lord now command thy servants, that are before thee, to seek out a man who is a skilful player on the harp; and it shall be, when the evil spirit from God cometh upon thee, that he shall play with his hand, and thou shalt be well.' And Saul said unto his servants: 'Provide me now a man that can play well, and bring him to me.' Then answered one of the young men, and said: 'Behold, I have seen a son of Jesse the Beth-lehemite, that is skilled in playing, and a mighty man of valour, and a man of war, and prudent in affairs, and a comely person, and the Lord is with him.' Wherefore Saul sent messages unto Jesse, and said: 'Send me David thy son, who is with the sheep.' And Jesse took an ass laden with bread, and a bottle of wine, and a kid and sent them by David his son unto Saul. And David came to Saul, and stood before him; and he loved him greatly; and he became his armour-bearer. And Saul sent to Jesse, saying: 'Let David, I pray thee, stand before me; for he hath found favour in my sight.' And it came to pass, when the evil spirit from God was upon Saul, that David took the harp and played with his hand; so Saul found relief, and it was well with him, and the evil spirit departed from him.

First Samuel 16:14-23

Like Pythagoras, he is said to have cured madmen by music.

Xenocrates (396-314 B.C.)

Placing the Mother of the Three Worlds upon a golden throne, studded with precious gems, Shulapani dances on the heights of Kailasa, and all the Gods gather round him:

Sarasvati plays on the *vina*, Indra on the flute, Brahma holds the time marking cymbals, Lakshmi begins a song, Vishnu plays on a drum, and all the gods stand round about:

Gandharvas, Yakshas, Patagas, Uragas, Suddhas, Sadhyas, Vidyadharas, Amaras, Apsarases, and all the beings dwelling in three worlds assemble there to witness the celestial dance and hear the music of the divine choir at the hour of twilight.

Shiva Pradosha Stotra

How greatly did I weep in Thy hymns and canticles, deeply moved by the voices of Thy sweet-speaking church! The voices flowed into mine ears, and the truth was poured forth into my heart, whence the agitation of my piety overflowed, and my tears ran over, and blessed was I therein.

St. Augustine (?-604) Confessions

I deem music worthy of praise, since it is the eldest of the arts, invented before the flood and once held in high esteem among the Greeks. Nor was it believed that anyone was learned enough, unless he was especially trained in music.

Adam of Dulda (fl. 1490) Musica

Finally one sister has awakened the other. Lately your music has stimulated my poetry to vigor and sprightliness after a long sleep of two years; even when I was still drunk with sleep, your music caused my madrigal to bubble forth in praise of Saint Hyacinth. I will endeavor to produce others, if possible, to the honor of our father, Saint Benedict, so that your harmonious spirit will have an edifying goal.

Abbot Angelo Grillo (c. 1550-1629) Letter to Padre Don Serafino Cantone

For he had been advised to make me relish science and duty by an unforced will and by my own desire, and to educate my mind in all liberty and gentleness without any severity or constraint. He did this so scrupulously that, because some maintain that it troubles the tender brains of children to wake them in the morning with a start and to snatch them suddenly and violently from sleep (wherein they are much more profoundly plunged than we), he caused me to be wakened by the sound of some musical instrument, and I was never without a man for that purpose.

Michel de Montaigne (1533-92) Of the Education of Children

Do you know that our soul is composed of harmony.

Leonardo da Vinci (1452-1519) Notebooks

The captain showed us the queen, attended with her ladies and gentlemen in the second gallery. She looked young, though she was at least eighteen hundred years old; and was handsome, slender, and as fine as a queen, that is as hands could make her. He then said to us, It is not yet a fit time to speak to the queen; be you but mindful of her doings in the meanwhile.

You have kings in your world that fantastically pretend to cure some certain diseases; as for example scrofula or wens, swelled throats, nicknamed the king's evil, and quartan agues, only with a touch: now our queen cures all manner of diseases without so much as touching the sick, but barely with a song, according to the nature of the distemper. He then showed us a set of the organs, and said, that when it was touched by her, those miraculous cures were performed. The organ was indeed the strangest that ever eyes beheld; for the pipes were of cassia fistula in the cod; the top and cornice of guiacum; the bellows of rhubarb; the petals of turbith, and the clavier or keys of scammony.

While we were examining this wonderful new make of an organ, the leprous were brought in by her abstractors, spodizators, masticators, pregustics, tabachins, chachanins, neemanins, rabrebans, nercins, rozuins, nebidins, tearins, segamions, perarons, chasinins, sarins, soteins, aboth, enilins, archasdarpenins, mebins, chabourins, and other officers, for whom I want names; so she played them I do not know what sort of a tune, or sung, and they were all immediately cured.

François Rabelais (1494?-1553) Pantagruel

Speake it not, answered the Count. For I shall enter in a large sea of the praise of Musicke, and call to rehearsall how much it hath alwaies beene renowned among them of olde time, and counted a holy matter: and how it hath beene the opinion of most wise Philosophers, that the worlde is made of musike, and the heavens in their moving make a melodie, and our soule is framed after the verie same sort and therefore lifteth up it selfe, and (as it were) reviveth the vertues and force of it selfe with Musicke.

Wherefore it is written that Alexander was so fervently stirred with it, that (in a manner) against his will hee was forced to arise from bankets and runne to weapon, afterward the Musition chaunging the stroke, and his manner of tune, pacified him selfe again, and returned from weapon to banketing.

And I shall tell you that grave Socrates when he was well stricken in yeares, learned to play upon the harpe. And I remember I have under stoode that Plato and Aristotle will have a man that is wel brought up, to be also a Musition: and declare with infinite reasons the force of musicke to bee to very great purpose in us, and for many causes (that should be too long to rehearse) ought necessarily to be learned from a mans childhood, not onely for the superficiall melodie that is heard, but to be a sufficient to bring into us a new habite that is good, and a custome inclining to vertue, which maketh the minde more apt to the conceiving of felicitie, even as bodely exercise maketh the bodie more lustie, and not onely hurteth not civil matters and warrelike affaires, but is a great stay to them.

Also Lycurgus in his sharp lawes allowed musicke. And it is read that the Lacedemonias, which were valiant in armes, and the Cretenses used harpes, and other soft instruments: and many most excellent Captaines of olde time (as Epaminondas) gave themselves to musicke: and such as had not a sight in it (as Themistocles) were a great deale the lesse set by.

Have you not reade, that among the first instructions which the good olde man Chiron taught Achilles in his tender age, whom he had brought up from his nurse and cradle, musicke was one? And the wise maister woulde have those handes that should shedde so much Troyan bloud, to bee often times occupied in playing upon the Harpe?

What souldier is there (therefore) that will thinke it a shame to follow Achilles, omitting many other famous Captaines that I could alledge?

Doe ye not then deprive our Courtier of Musicke, which doth not onely make sweete the mindes of men, but also many times wilde beastes tame: and who so savoureth it not, a man may assuredly thinke him not to be well in his wits.

Behold I pray you what force it hath, that in times past allured a fish to suffer a man to ride upon it through the tempestuous sea.

We may see it used in the holy temples, to render laud and thankes unto God, and it is a credible matter that it is acceptable unto him, and that he hath given it unto us for a most sweete lightning of our travailes and vexations.

So that many times the boysterous labours in the fields, in the heat of the sun, beguile their paine with rude and caterly singing.

With this the unmannerly countrie woman, that ariseth before day out of her sleepe to spinne and carde, defendeth her selfe and maketh her labour pleasant.

This is the most sweete pastime after raine, winde and tempest, unto the miserable marriners.

With this doe the verie Pilgrimes comfort themselves in their troublesome and long voyages. And oftentimes prisoners, in adversitie, fetters and in stockes.

In like manner for a greater proofe, that the tunableenesse of musick (though it be but rude) is a verie great refreshing of all worldlye paines and grifes, a man woulde judge that nature hath taught it unto nurses for a speciall remedie to the continuall waylings of sucking babes, which at the sound of their voice fall into a quiet and sweete sleepe, forgetting the teares that are so proper to them, and given us of nature in that age, for a gesse of the rest of our life to come.

Baldassare Castiglione (1478-1529) Book of the Courtier

Abundance of people of the best rank and quality being shut up in the city, namely, lords, knights, and gentlemen of the countries round about, besides the souldiers and citizens, who, all or most of them, came constantly every Sunday to hear public prayers and sermon, the number was so exceeding great, that the church was (as I may say) even cramming and squeezing full. Now here you must take notice that they had then a custom in that church (which I hear not of in any other Cathedral which was) that always before the sermon, the whole congregation sang a psalm, together with the quire and the organ; and you must also know, that there was then a most excellent-large-plump-lusty-full-speaking organ which cost (as I am credibly informed) a thousand pounds. This organ I say, (when the psalm was set before the sermon), being let out into all its fullness of stops, together with the quire, began the psalm. But when the vast-conchording-unity of the whole congregation-chorus, came (as I may say) thundering in, even so it made the very ground shake under us; (oh the unutterable ravishing soul's delight!) in which I was so transported, and wrapt up into high contemplation, that there was no room left in my whole man, namely, body and spirit, for anything below divine and heavenly raptures.

Thomas Mace (1620-c. 1710) Music's Monument

50
In Praise of Music

The Force of Musick is more wonderful than the Conveyance. How strangely does it awaken the Mind! It infuses an unexpected vigour, makes the impression agreeable and sprightly, and seems to furnish a new Capacity as well as a new opportunity of Satisfaction. Have you not observed a Captain at the Head of a Company, how much he is altered at the Beat of a Drum? What a vigorous Motion, what an erected Posture, what an enterprising Visage, all of a suddain? His blood charges in his veins, his Spirits jump like Gunpowder, and seem impatient to attack the Enemy.

Jeremy Collier (1650-1726) An Essay of Musick

Rabbi Pinhas always spoke in high praise of music and song. Once he said: "Lord of the world, if I could sing, I should not let you remain up above. I should harry you with my song until you came down and stayed here with us."

Tales of the Hasidim Translated by Martin Buber

With my wife to the King's House to see 'The Virgin Marys,' the first time it hath been acted a great while: and it is mighty pleasant; not that the play is worth much, but it is finely acted by Beck Marshall. But that which did please me beyond any thing in the whole world, was the wind-musique when the angel comes down; which is so sweet that it ravished me, and indeed, in a word, did wrap up my soul so that it made me really sick, just

as I have formerly been when in love with my wife; that neither then, nor all the evening going home, and at home, was I able to think of anything, but remained all night transported, so as I could not believe that ever any musique hath that real command over the soul of man as this did upon me; and makes me resolve to practice wind-musique, and to make my wife do the like.

Samuel Pepys (1633-1703) Diary

You will stare at a strange notion of mine. If it appears even a mad one, do not wonder. Had I children, my utmost endeavors should be to make them musicians. Considering I have no ear, nor even thought of music, the preference seems odd, and yet it is embraced on frequent recollection. In short, as my aim would be to make them happy, I think it is the most probable method. It is a resource which will last them their lives, unless they grow deaf; it depends upon themselves, not on others; always amuses and soothes, if not consoles, and of all fashionable pleasures is the cheapest. It is capable of fame without danger of criticism, is susceptible of enthusiasm without being priest-ridden; and, unlike other mortal passions, is sure of being gratified in heaven.

Horace Walpole (1717-1797)

I must study politics and war that my sons may have liberty to study mathematics and philosophy . . . in order to give their children a right to study painting, poetry and music.

John Adams (1735-1826)

In the evening, our gentleman-farmer, and two others entertained themselves and the company with a great number of tunes on the fiddle. John-

son desired to have 'Let ambition fire thy mind' played over again, and appeared to give a patient attention to it; though he owned to me that he was very insensible to the power of music. I told him that it affected me to such a degree as often to agitate my nerves painfully, producing in my mind alternate sensations of pathetic dejection, so that I was ready to shed tears; and of daring resolution, so that I was inclined to rush into the thickest part of the battle. 'Sir' said he, 'I should never hear it if it made me such a fool.'

James Boswell (1740-95) Life of Johnson

My childhood's heart was to my dreams a sea of music, whereon floated picture-boats.

Hans C. Andersen (1805-75) The Improvisatore

Music hath caught a higher pace than any virtue that I know. It is the arch-reformer.

Henry David Thoreau (1817-1862) Journal

When I hear music, I fear no danger. I am invulnerable. I see no foe. I am related to the earliest times and to the latest.

Henry David Thoreau (1817-1862) Journal

When I hear music, it seems to me that all the sins of my life pass slowly by me with veiled faces, and lay their hands on my head and say softly, My Child.

Sidney Lanier (1842-81) On Music

I would believe only in a God that knew how to dance.

Friedrich Nietzsche (1844-1900) Thus Spake Zarathustra

Mr. Weir has told me of the case of a bullfinch which had been taught to pipe a German waltz, and who was so good a performer that he cost ten guineas; when the bird was first introduced into a room where other birds were kept and he began to sing, all the others, consisting of about twenty linnets and canaries, ranged themselves on the nearest side of their cages and listened with the greatest interest to the new performer.

Charles Darwin (1809-1882) Descent of Man

Every impulse and spring of art seems to have died in me, except for music, and that I pursue under almost an impossibility of getting on.

Gerard M. Hopkins (1844-1899) Letter to Robert Bridges

. . . . I groped in my soul's very viscera for the tune and thrummed the sweetest and most secret catgut of the mind.

Gerard M. Hopkins (1844-1899) Letter to Robert Bridges

I certainly believe I could make a better musician than many who profess to be, and are accepted as such. Mark, I do not for a moment call myself a musician, nor do I suspect I ever shall be, but there! I love Music, with such *strength* that I have had to conceal the passion, for fear it be thought weakness.

Wilfred Owen (1893-1918) Diary

I won't be my father's Jack
I won't be my mother's Jill,
I will be the fiddler's wife
And have music when I will.

T'other little tune,
T'other little tune
Prithee, love, play me
T'other little tune.

Nursery Rhyme

Music does various things to me. First and foremost, it liberates trains of thoughts. Then it encourages musing and daydreaming. Best of all, it conjures up worlds of marvelous possibility, conditions of ecstasy, visions of magical radiance of a universe permeated by divinely intelligent goodness, and of a Beyond surpassing all present powers of imagination.

Only the greatest poetry, the noblest architecture, the sublimest scenery can compete with music in arousing such feelings. And it is perhaps more poignant, more penetrating, more permeating than any of them, or all of them put together. It certainly is more transporting.

Bernard Berenson (1865-1959) Rumor and Reflection

Meanwhile nobody ever dreamt of teaching me anything. At fifteen, when the family broke up, I could neither play nor read a note of music. Whether you choose to put it that I was condemned to be a critic or saved from being an executant, the fact remains that when the house became musicless, I was forced to teach myself how to play written music on the piano from a book with a diagram of the keyboard in it or else be starved of music.

George Bernard Shaw (1856-1900) Preface to London Music in 1888-89 as Heard by Corno di Bassetto

Sing your song looking up at the sky.

Words for an American Indian Song

Music is like a bewitched sweetheart to me. Famous as a painter, writer or modern composer? Bad joke. As it is, I am without a profession and loaf.

Paul Klee (1879-1940) Diary

I loved music more than anything else, and I loved Scriabin more than anyone else in the world of music. I began to lisp in music not long before my first acquaintance with him. On his return I was the pupil of a composer even now alive and well. I had only to go through orchestration. All sorts of things were said, but the only important thing is that even if only antagonistic things had been said I could not imagine a life not lived in music.

Boris Pasternak (1890-1960) Safe Conduct

The Composer Speaks

Reasons briefly set down by the author to persuade everyone to learn to sing.

1. First it is a knowledge easily taught, and quickly learned; where there is a good master, and an apt scholar.

2. The exercise of singing is delightful to nature, and good to preserve health.

3. It doth strengthen all the parts of the breast, and doth open the pipes.

4. It is a singular good remedy for a stuttering and stammering in the speech.

5. It is the best means to procure a perfect pronunciation, and to make a good orator.

6. It is the only way to know where Nature hath bestowed the benefit of a good voice; which gift is so rare, as there is not one among a thousand that hath it: and in many, that excellent gift is lost, because they want art to express Nature.

7. There is not any music of instruments whatsoever comparable to that which is made of the voices of men; where the voices are good, and the same well sorted or ordered.

8. The better the voice is, the meeter it is to honour and serve God there-with: and the voice of man is chiefly to be employed to that end.

Omnis spiritus laudet Dominum
Since singing is so good a thing
I wish all men would learn to sing.

William Byrd (1543?-1623) Psalms, Sonnets and Songs of Sadness and Piety

Musick is the exaltation of poetry. Both of them may excell apart, but surely they are most excellent when they are joyn'd, because nothing is then wanting to either of their proportions; for thus they appear like wit and beauty in the same person.

Henry Purcell (1659-1695) Preface to Dioclesian

Figured bass is the most perfect foundation of music. It is executed with both hands in such a manner that the left hand plays the notes that are written, while the right adds consonances and dissonances thereto, making an agreeable harmony for the glory of God and the justifiable gratification of the soul. Like all music, the figured bass should have no other end and aim than the glory of the God and the recreation of the soul; where this is not kept in mind there is no true music, but only an infernal clamour and ranting.

Johann Sebastian Bach (1685-1750)

Gentlemen,

It was indeed a most pleasant surprise to receive such a flattering letter from a part of the world where I could never have imagined that the products of my poor talents were known. But when I see that not only is my name familiar to you, but my compositions are performed by you with approval and satisfaction, the warmest wishes of my heart are fulfilled: to be considered a not wholly unworthy priest of this sacred art where my works are known. You reassure me on this point as regards your fatherland, but even more, you happily persuade me—and this cannot fail to be a real source of consolation to me in my declining years—that I am often the enviable means by which you, and so many other families sensible to heartfelt emotion, derive, in their homely circle, their pleasure—their enjoyment. How reassuring this thought is to me!—Often, when struggling

Menuet.

against the obstacles of every sort which oppose my labours; often, when the powers of mind and body weakened, and it was difficult for me to continue in the course I had entered on;—a secret voice whispered to me: "There are so few happy and contented peoples here below; grief and sorrow are always their lot; perhaps your labours will once be a source from which the care-worn, or the man burdened with affairs, can derive a few moments' rest and refreshment." This was indeed a powerful motive to press onwards, and this is why I now look back with a cheerful satisfaction on the labours expended on this art, to which I have devoted so many long years of uninterrupted effort and exertion. And now I thank you in the fullness of my heart for your kindly thoughts of me, and beg you to forgive me for delaying my answer so long: enfeebled health, and inseparable companion of the grey-haired septuagenarian and pressing business deprived me till now of this pleasure. Perhaps nature may yet grant me the joy of composing a little memorial for you, from which you may gather the feelings of a gradually dying veteran, who would fain even after his death survive in the charming circle of which you draw so wonderful a picture. I have the honour to be, with profound respect,

Your wholly obedient servant,
Joseph Haydn (1732-1809)
Letter to Jean Phillip Kruger

To enjoy the effects of music fully, we must completely lose ourselves in it; to judge it, we must relate it to the source through which we are affected by it. This source is nature. Nature endows us with the feeling that moves us in all our musical experiences; we might call her gift *instinct*. Let us allow instinct to inform our judgements, let us see what mysteries it unfolds to us before we pronounce our verdicts and if there are still men sufficiently self-assured to dare make judgements on their own authority, there is reason to hope that none will be found weak enough to listen to them.

Jean Philippe Rameau (1683-1764) Observations sur Notre Instinct pour la Musique et sur son Principe

. . . . Moreover, as Papa is well aware, there are also *opere buffe* here and there in the spring, summer and autumn, which one can write for practice and for something to do. I should not make very much, it is true, but all the same, it would be something; and they would bring me more honour and credit than if I were to give a hundred concerts in Germany. And I am happier when I have something to compose, for that, after all, is my sole delight and passion.

Wolfgang Amadeus Mozart (1756-1791) Letter to his Father

Music . . . must never offend the ear; it must please the hearer, in other words, it must never cease to be music.

Wolfgang Amadeus Mozart (1756-1791) Letter to his Father

. . . what a humiliation when one stood beside me and heard a flute in the distance and *I heard nothing*, or someone heard *the shepherd singing* and again I heard nothing, such incidents brought me to the verge of despair, but little more and I would have put an end to my life—only art it was that withheld me, ah it seemed impossible to leave the world until I produced all that I felt called upon to produce, and so I endured this wretched existence...

Ludwig van Beethoven (1770-1827) Heiligenstadt Testament

The description of a picture belongs to the field of painting; in this the poet can count himself more fortunate than my muse for his territory is not so restricted as mine in this respect, though mine, on the other hand, extends into other regions, and my dominion is not easily reached.

Ludwig van Beethoven (1770-1827) Letter to Wilhelm Gerhard

What love is to man, music is to the arts and mankind. Music is love itself —it is the purest, most ethereal language of passion, showing in a thousand ways all possible changes of color and feelings; and though only true in a single instance, it can be understood by thousands of men—who all feel differently.

Karl Maria von Weber (1786-1826)

I am in the world only for the purpose of composing.

Franz Schubert (1797-1828)

Which of the two powers, love or music, is able to lift man to the sublimest heights? It is a great question, but it seems to me that one might answer it thus: love cannot express the idea of music, while music may give an idea

Concert Méchanique
Inventé par R.ᵉ Richard,
Exposé à la Biblioteq. du Roi
17   69

Dédié à Monseigneur Le ———— Comte de Saint Florentin,
Ministre & Secretaire d'État Com- ———— mandeur, Chancelier & Surintendant
des Ordres du Roi . ———— Par Son très-humble et très-obéissant Serviteur Richard.

of love. Why separate the one from the other? They are the two wings of the soul.

Hector Berlioz (1803-1869) Memoires

No children can be brought to healthy manhood on sweetmeats and pastry. Spiritual like bodily nourishment must be simple and solid. The masters have provided it; cleave to them.

Robert Schumann (1810-1856) Aphorisms

The study of the history of music and the hearing of masterworks of different epochs will speediest of all cure you of vanity and self-adoration.

Robert Schumann (1810-1856) Aphorisms

Music speaks the most universal of languages, that through which the soul finds itself inspired in a free, indefinite manner, and yet feels itself at home.

Robert Schumann (1810-1856) Aphorisms

People often complain that music is too ambiguous; that what they should think when they hear it is so unclear, whereas everyone understands words. With me it is exactly the reverse, and not only with regard to an entire speech, but also with individual words. These, too, seem to me so ambiguous, so vague, so easily misunderstood in comparison with genuine music, which fills the soul with a thousand things better than words.

Felix Mendelssohn (1890-1847) Letter to Mar-Andre Souchay

I naturally have no special ambition to see my poetry cast into the shade by my music, but I would certainly be guilty of a lie were I to pretend that my music was at the mercy of my poetry. I cannot make use of any poetic matter that is not first conditioned by music.

Richard Wagner (1813-1883) Letter to Eduard Hanslick

It is the province of the present-day dramatist to give expression and spiritual meaning to the material interests of our own times, but to the operatic poet and composer falls the task of conjuring up the holy spirit of poetry as it comes down to us in the sagas and legends of past ages. For music affords a medium of synthesis which the poet alone, particularly in association with the stage, has not at command.

Richard Wagner (1813-1883) Letter to Karl Gaillard

You ask whether I had a particular program in mind when I composed this symphony. I generally reply to questions of this sort about my symphonic works: nothing of the sort. Actually it is extremely difficult to answer this question. How can one interpret those vague feelings which course through one during the composition of an instrumental work, without reference to a definite subject? It is a purely lyrical process. A sort of confession of the soul in music; an accumulation of material flowing forth again in notes just as the lyric poet pours himself out in verse. The difference is that music possesses much richer means of expression and is a more subtle medium for translating the thousand shifting moments of the feelings of the soul.

Piotr Ilyich Tchaikovsky (1840-1893) Letter to Nadezhda Filaretovna von Meck

I haven't the honour of knowing the organist who is entrusted with providing harmonious music for the congregation at Saint-Philippe, but I shall

certainly undertake to write the two hundred bars you ask me for. If they do not turn out to be very beautiful, they will at least express my friendly feelings and also attempt at conveying feeling that I have not expressed before. I don't know whether it will be strictly nuptial; the trouble is that I've been living in sin with Music for too long. . . .

Claude Debussy (1862-1918) Letter to Pierre Louys

71
The Composer Speaks

Gather impressions. But don't hurry to note them down; for music has this over painting, that it can bring together all manner of variations of colour and light. It is a point that is not often observed though it is quite obvious.

And then, from time to time forget music altogether. "Practice makes perfect" is a schoolmaster's notion. And it is not in very good taste to badger those one loves the most with constant requests.

Claude Debussy (1862-1918) Letter to Pierre Louys

He who does not take a thorough pleasure in a simple chord progression well constructed, beautiful in its arrangement does not love music; he who does not prefer the first "Prelude" in the Well-Tempered Clavier played without nuances as the composer wrote it for the instrument, to the same prelude embellished with a passionate melody, does not love music; he who does not prefer a folk tune of a lovely character, or a Gregorian chant without any accompaniment to a series of dissonant and pretentious chords does not love music.

Charles Camille Saint-Saëns (1835-1921) Ecole buissonnière

. . . be it laughter or tears, feverish passion or religious ecstasy, nothing, in the category of human feelings, is a stranger to music . . .

Paul Dukas (1865-1935) Revue Hebdomadaire

I feel strongly that the great fundamentals should be more discussed in all public meetings, and also in meetings of schools and colleges, not only the students but also the faculty should get down to more thinking and action about the great problems which concern all countries and all people in the world today, and not let the politicians do it all and have the whole say.

I have often been told that it is not the function of music (or a concert) to concern itself with matters like these. But I do not by any means agree. I think that it is *one* of the things that music can do, if it happens to want to, if it comes naturally, and is not the result of superimposition—I have had some fights about this.

Charles Ives (1874-1954) Letter to Lehman Engel

If one wishes to make music, one should not paint or write poetry or desire to describe anything. But what one makes music out of is still the whole— that is the feeling, thinking, breathing, suffering human being. There would be no objection to a "program" (though this may not be exactly the highest step on the ladder) provided that it is a *musician* who is expressing himself in it and not a writer, philosopher, or painter (all of these being contained in the musician).

Gustav Mahler (1860-1911) Letter to Bruno Walter

The whole life of a man is in the folk music—body, soul, environment, everything. He who grows out of folk music makes a whole man of himself. Folk music binds people together, linking them with other peoples and uniting mankind with a spiritual bond of happiness and blessing.

Leoš Janáček (1854-1928)

As for myself, I experience a sort of terror when, at the moment of setting to work and finding myself before the infinitude of possibilities that present themselves, I have the feeling that everything is permissible to me. If everything is permissible to me, the best and the worst; if nothing offers me any resistance, then my effort is inconceivable, and I cannot use anything as a basis, and consequently every undertaking becomes futile.

Will I then have to lose myself in this abyss of freedom? To what shall I cling in order to escape the dizziness that seizes me before the virtuality of this infinitude? However, I shall not succumb. I shall overcome my terror and shall be reassured by the thought that I have the seven notes of the scale and its chromatic intervals at my disposal, that strong and weak accents are within my reach, and that in all of these I possess solid and concrete elements which offer me a field of experience just as vast as the upsetting and dizzy infinitude that had just frightened me. It is into this field that I shall sink my roots, fully convinced that combinations which have at their disposal twelve sounds in each octave and all possible rhythmic varieties promise me riches that all the activity of human genius will never exhaust.

Igor Stravinsky (1882-   ) Poetics of Music

What I love about jazz is that it's "blue" and you don't care.

Erik Satie (1866-1925)

To a humanity looking for elements of hope, music ought to be an important matter. We may even say that man will begin to recover the moment he takes art as seriously as physics, chemistry or money. There is no other human activity that asks for such a harmonious cooperation of "intellect" and "soul" as artistic creation and, especially, music (I do not say this only because I am a musician! I have very good reasons to say so!). Music is human. Music is also extra-human inasmuch as it is a mirror of universal laws. To destructive analysis music opposes synthesis. To the uniformization of science, which reduces qualities to quantities, music opposes a hier-

archy of values. *Our mechanized minds need to be musicalized.* We have developed only half of man's possibilities, or rather, have developed that half completely out of proportion to the other half. We have deified the intellect, we have separated it completely from the other side of human nature. We must seek a synthesis. Music as an art and as a science can do it. This is not a petty problem. It is *the* problem of our time.

Ernst Lévy (1895-   ) Letter to Barnett Byman

75

The Composer Speaks

Jazz is the result of the energy stored up in America. It is a very energetic kind of music, noisy, boisterous and even vulgar. One thing is certain. Jazz has contributed an enduring value to America in the sense that it has expressed ourselves. It is an original American achievement which will endure, not as jazz perhaps, but which will leave its mark on future music in one form or another.

George Gershwin (1898-1937)

Music is in a continual state of becoming.

Aaron Copland (1900-   ) Music and the Imagination

Most people use music as a couch; they want to be pillowed on it, relaxed and consoled for the stress of daily living. But serious music was never meant to be soporific. Contemporary music, especially, is created to wake you up, not put you to sleep. It is meant to stir and excite you—it may even exhaust you. But isn't that the kind of stimulation you go to theater or read a book for? Why make an exception of music?

Aaron Copland (1900-   )

As a composer, I had a slump for the first year of the war, feeling that writing music was about the most futile occupation. What got me out of it chiefly was getting letters from men in the armed forces who said they hoped I was keeping on composing because that was one of the things they were out there for.

Walter Piston (1894-   ) Letter to Arthur Berger

Emotion is specific, individual, and conscious; music goes deeper than this, to the energies which animate our psychic life, and out of these creates a pattern which has an existence, laws, and human significance of its own. It reproduces for us the most intimate essence, the tempo and the energy, of our spiritual being; our tranquillity and our restlessness, our animation and our discouragement, our vitality and our weakness—all, in fact, of the fine shades of dynamic variation of our inner life. It reproduces these far more directly and more specifically than is possible through any other medium of human communication.

Roger Sessions (1896-   ) The Composer and His Message

I believe that some day we shall be weary of this daily miserable struggle, that a little true love will be born in the withered hearts of men. Perhaps, after our hatred, kindled only by a few, there will come one of those cleansing revolutions that will shake the world on its foundations and sweep away the poisonous vapors. Perhaps, then, a new life will rise up and with it something of youth and verdure and joy; while the old limping religions, the gods in whom no one believes, will be swept away with the ruins. . . . A little fraternity, a little love, a little gladness will gleam on the face of the world, and catch up the hearts of men in one impulse, in one rhythm. And for these new hearts there will be need to be new songs.

Ernest Bloch (1880-1959)

IV

The Poet Speaks

Rejoice in the Lord, O ye righteous
Praise is comely for the upright.
Give thanks unto the Lord with harp,
Sing praises unto Him with the psaltery
    of ten strings.
Sing unto Him a new song;
Play skilfully amid shouts of joy.

Psalms 33:1-3

    Hallelujah.
Praise God in His sanctuary;
Praise Him in the firmament of His power.
Praise Him for His mighty acts;
Praise Him according to His abundant greatness.
Praise Him with the blast of the horn;
Praise Him with the psaltery and harp.
Praise Him with the timbrel and dance;
Praise Him with stringed instruments and the pipe.

Praise Him with the loud-sounding cymbals;
Praise Him with the clanging cymbals.
Let every thing that hath breath praise the Lord.
Hallelujah.

Psalm 150

80
In Praise of Music

And be not drunk with wine, wherein is
excess; but be filled with the Spirit;
Speaking to yourselves in psalms and
hymns and spiritual songs, singing and
making melody in your heart to the Lord.

Ephesians 5:18

Is any among you afflicted? Let him pray.
Is any merry? let him sing psalms.

James 5:13

. . . . there was every kind of bird, brought under the spell of the singing,
and all beasts of the mountains and whatever feeds in the recesses of the
sea, and a horse stood entranced, held in control, not by a bridle, but by
the music, and a bull, having abandoned its pasturage was listening to the
strains of the lyre, and loins by nature fierce were being lulled to sleep in
response to its harmony. You could see the bronze taking the shape of
rivers flowing from their sources toward the singing, and a wave of the
sea raising itself aloft for love of the song, and rocks being smitten with
the sensation of music, and every plant in its season hastening from its
usual abode toward the music of Orpheus.

Callistratus (fl. 3rd century) Descriptions, VII: On the Statue of Orpheus
Translated by Arthur Fairbanks

Orpheus, son of the Thracian King Oeagrus and the Muse Calliope, was the most famous poet and musician whoever lived. Apollo presented him with a lyre, and the Muses taught him its use, so that he not only enchanted wild beasts, but made the trees and rocks move from their places to follow the sound of his music. At Zone in Thrace a number of ancient mountain oaks are still standing in the pattern of one of his dances, just as he left them.

First waiting until their husbands had entered Apollo's temple, where Orpheus served as priest, they seized the weapons stacked outside, burst in, murdered their husbands, and tore Orpheus limb from limb. His head they threw into the river Bebrus, but it floated, still singing, down to the sea, and was carried to the island of Lesbos.

Tearfully, the Muses collected his limbs and buried them at Leibethra, at the foot of Mount Olympus, where the nightingales now sing sweeter than anywhere else in the world. . . .

The Myth of Orpheus The Greek Myths by Robert Graves

ON HEARING TUNG PLAY THE FLAGEOLET

(A Poem to Palace-Attendant Fang)

When this melody for the flageolet was made Lady Ts'ai,
When long ago one by one she sang its eighteen stanzas,
Even the Tartars were shedding tears into the border-grasses,
And the envoy of China was heart-broken, turning back home
    with his escort.
. . . Cold fires now of old battles are grey on ancient forts,
And the wilderness is shadowed with white new-flying snow.
. . . When the player first brushes the Shang string and the
    Chueh and then the Yu,
Autumn-leaves in all four quarters are shaken with a murmur.
Tung, the master,
Must have been taught in heaven.

Demons come from the deep pine-wood and stealthily listen
To music slow, then quick, following his hand,
Now far away, now near again, according to his heart.
A hundred birds from an empty mountain scatter and return;
Three thousand miles of floating clouds darken and lighten;
A wildgoose fledgling, left behind, cries for its flock,
And a Tartar child for the mother he loves.
Then river waves are calmed
And birds are mute that were singing,
And Wu-chu tribes are homesick for their distant land,
And out of the dust of Siberian steppes rises a plaintive sorrow.
... Suddenly the low sound leaps to a freer tune,
Like a long wind swaying a forest, a downpour breaking tiles,
A cascade through the air, flying over tree-tops.
... A wild deer calls to his fellows. He is running among the mansions
In the corner of the capital by the Eastern Palace wall...
Phoenix Lake lies opposite the Gate of Green Jade;
But how can fame and profit concern a man of genius?
Day and night I long for him to bring his lute again.

Li Ch'i Translated by Witter Bynner

83 The Poet Speaks

ON HEARING CHUN
THE BUDDHIST MONK FROM SHU PLAY HIS LUTE

The monk from Shu with his green silk lute-case,
Walking west down O-mei Mountain,
Has brought me by one touch of the strings
The breath of pines in a thousand valleys.
I hear him in the cleansing brook,
I hear him in the icy bells;
And I feel no change though the mountain darkens
And cloudy autumn heaps the sky.

Li Po (c. 700-762 A.D.) Translated by Witter Bynner

84
In Praise of Music

Blind men, blind men
In the courtyard of Chou.
We have set up the cross-board, the stand,
With the upright hooks, the standing plumes.
The little and big drums are hung for beating;
The tambourines and stone-chimes, the mallet-
    box and scraper.
All is ready, and they play.
Pan-pipes and flute are ready and begin.
Sweetly blend the tones,
Solemn the melody of their bird-music.
The ancestors are listening;
As our guests they have come,
To gaze long upon their victories.

The Book of Songs Translated by Arthur Waley

THE SWAN AND GOOSE

A rich man bought a Swan and Goose—
That for song and this for use.
It chanced his simple-minded cook
One night the Swan for Goose mistook.
But in the dark about to chop
The Swan in two above the crop,
He heard the lyric note, and stayed
The action of the fatal blade.

And thus we see a proper tune
Is sometimes very opportune.

Aesop (6th century B.C.) Translated by William Ellery Leonard

So sang the bard illustrious; then his robe
Of purple dye with both hand o'er his head
Ulysses drew, behind its ample folds
Veiling his face, through fear to be observed
By the Phaeacians weeping at the song;
And ever as the bard harmonious ceased,
He wiped his tears, and, drawing from his brows
The mantle, pour'd libations to the Gods.
But when the Chiefs (for they delighted heard
Those sounds) solicited again the bard,
And he renew'd the strain, then cov'ring close
His count'nance, as before, Ulysses wept.

Homer (c. 10th century B.C.) The Odyssey Translated by William Cowper

The gloom of death is on the raven's wing,
    The song of death is in the raven's cries:
But when Demophilus begins to sing,
    The raven dies.

Nicharchus Translated by Edwin Arlington Robinson

O lyre of gold, Apollo's
Treasure, shared with the violet-wreathed Muses,
The light foot hears you, and the brightness begins:

Your notes compel the singer
When to lead out the dance
The prelude is sounded on your trembling strings.
You quench the warrior Thunderbolt's everlasting flame:

On God's sceptre the Eagle sleeps,
Dropping his swift wings on either side.

Pindar (c. 518-422 B.C.) The Power of Music Translated by H. T. Wade-Gery and
C. M. Bowra

87
The Poet Speaks

And yet this were surely a gain, to heal men's
wounds by music's spell...

Euripides (5th century B.C.) Medea

Others say that Orpheus said: generals invite me to banquets that they
may delight themselves from me: I nonetheless take my delight from them,
since, in what direction I wish, I can bend their souls, from anger to pardon,
from sadness to joy, from greed to generosity, from fear to bravery.

Constantinus Africanus (c. 1020-1087)

Dan he took out his pipes to play
Bit sair his hert wi dol and wae

And first he played da notes on noy
An dan he played de notes o joy.

An den he played de god gabler reel
Dat meicht ha made a sick hert hale.

Scottish Popular Ballad

... sometimes a wild warrior would harp joy, touch the
gleewood; sometimes would tell a song true and sorrowful...

Beowulf

I have learned my songs from the music of many
birds, from the music of many waters.

Poet of the Kalevala

THE HARP OF CNOC I CHOSGAIR

Harp of Cnoc I Chosgair, you who bring sleep to eyes long
sleepless; sweet, subtle, plangent, gald, cooling, grave.

Excellent instrument with the smooth gentle curve, crying
out under red fingers, musicians that have charmed us, red,
lion-like, of full melody.

You who lure the bird from the flock, you who refresh the
mind, brown spotted one of sweet words; ardent, wondrous,
passionate.

You who heal every wounded warrior, joy and allurement to
women, familiar guide over the dark blue water, mystic sweet-
sounding music.

You who silence every instrument of music, yourself a pleasing
plaintive instrument, dweller among the Race of Conn, instrument
yellow-brown and firm.

The one darling of the skilled, restless, smooth, of sweet tune,
purple star above the fairy hills, breast-jewel of High Kings.

Sweet tender flowers, brown harp of Diarmaid, shape not unloved
by hosts, voice of the cuckoos in May!

I have not heard of music ever such as your frame makes since
the time of the fairy people, fair brown many-coloured bough,
gentle, wide-shouldered, glorious.

Sound of the calm wave on the beach, pure shadowing tree of
true music, carousals are drunk in your company, voice of the
swan over shining streams.

Cry of the fairy women from the Hill of Ler, no melody can
match you, every house is sweet-stringed through your guidance,
you the pinnacle of harp-music. . . .

Gofraidh Fionn O Dalaigh (c. 1385)

THE SECRETE WORKING OF MUSICK

What the secrete working of Musick is in the myndes of men, as well appeareth hereby, that some of the auncient Philosophers, and those the moste wise, as Plato and Pythagoras, held for opinion, that the mind was made of a certaine harmonie and musicall nombers, for the great compassion, and likeness of affection in thone and in the other, as also by that memorable history of Alexander: to whom when as Timotheus the great Musitian playd the Phrygian melody, it is said, that he was distraught with such unwonted fury, that, streightway rysing from the table in great rage, he caused himselfe to be armed, as ready to goe to warre, (for that musick is very warlike.) And immediatly when as the Musitian chaunged his stroke into the Lydian and Ionique harmony, he was so furr from warring, that he sat as styl, as if he had bene in matters of counsell. Such might is in musick: wherefore Plato and Aristotle forbid the Acardian Melodie from children and youth. For that being altogether on the fyft and vii tone, it is of great force to molifie and quench the kindly courage, which useth to burne in yong brests. So that it is not incredible which the Poete here sayth, that Musick can breave the soule of sence.

Edmund Spenser (1552?-99) The Secrete Working of Musick

Where gripying grief the hart would wound and dolfull
    domps the minde oppresse
There Musick with her siluer sound, is wont with
    spede to giue redresse,
Of troubled minde for euery sore, swete Musick hath
    a salue therefore.

In ioye it make our mirth abound, in grief it chers
    our heauy sprights,
The carefull head release hath found, by Musicks
    pleasant swete delights

Our sences, what should I saie more, are subiect vnto
    Musicks lore.

The Godds by Musick hath their praie, the foule
    therein doeth ioye,
For as the Romaine Poets saie, in seas whom Pirats
    would destroye
A Dolphin saued from death moste sharpe, Arion
    plaiying on his harpe.

A heauenly gift, that turned the minde, like as the
    stern doth rule the ship,
Musick whom the Gods assignde to comfort man,
    whom cares would nip,
Sith thou both man and beast doest moue, what wiseman
    then wil thee reproue.

Richard Edwards (1523?-66) Quoted by Peter in Romeo and Juliet

. . . music as the sweetness and, as it were, the soul of poetry.

Torquato Tasso (1544-95)

How silver-sweet sound lovers' tongues by night,
Like softest music to attending ears!

William Shakespeare (1564-1616) Romeo and Juliet

JESSICA: I am never merry when I hear sweet music.

LORENZO: The reason is, your spirits are attentive.
        For do but note a wild and wanton herd,
        Or race of youthful and unhandled colts,

Fetching mad bounds, bellowing and neighing
    loud,
Which is the hot condition of their blood;
If they but hear perchance a trumpet sound,
Or any air of music touch their ears,
You shall perceive them make a mutual stand,
Their savage eyes turned to a modest gaze
By the sweet power of music. Therefore the poet
Did feign that Orpheus drew trees, stones, and
    floods;
Since naught so stockish, hard and full of rage,
But music for the time doth change his nature.
That man that hath no music in himself,
Nor is not moved with concord of sweet sounds,
Is fit for treasons, stratagems, and spoils;
The motions of his spirit are dull as night,
And his affections dark as Erebus.
Let no such man be trusted. Mark the music.

William Shakespeare (1564-1616) The Merchant of Venice

92
In Praise of Music

PERICLES: Give me my robes. I am wild in my beholding.
            O heavens bless my girl! But, hark, what music?
            Tell Helicanus, my Marina, tell him
            O'er, point by point, for yet he seems to doubt,
            How sure you are my daughter. But, what music?

PERICLES: My lord, I hear none.

PERICLES: None!
            The music of the spheres! List, my Marina.

PERICLES: It is not good to cross him; give him way.

HELICANUS: Rarest sounds! Do ye not hear?

LYSIMACHUS: Music, my lord? I hear.

LYSIMACHUS: Most heavenly music!
It nips me unto listening, and thick slumber
Hangs upon my eyes. Let me rest.

LYSIMACHUS: A pillow for his head.
So, leave him all.

William Shakespeare (1564-1616) Pericles

Music to hear, why hear'st thou music sadly?
Sweets with sweets war not, joy delights in joy:
Why lovest thou that which thou receivest not
   gladly,
Or else receivest with pleasure thine annoy?
If the true concord of well-tuned sounds
By unions married, do offend thine ear,
They do but sweetly chide thee, who confounds
In singleness the parts that thou shouldst bear.
Mark how one string, sweet husband to another,
Strikes each in each by mutual ordering;
Resembling sire and child and happy mother,
Who, all in one, one pleasing note do sing:
   Whose speechless song, being many, seeming
      one,
   Sings this to thee: 'Thou single wilt prove
      none.'

William Shakespeare (1564-1616) Sonnet, viii

The setting-sun, and music at the close,
As the last taste of sweets, is sweetest last,
Writ in remembrance more than things long past.

William Shakespeare (1564-1616) Richard II

He that would his body keep
From diseases must not weep;
But whoever laughs and sings,
Never he his body brings
Into fever, gouts, or rheums.

Fras. Beaumont (1584-1616) and J. Fletcher (1576-1625)

GRATIANA DANCING AND SINGING

See! with what constant motion,
Even and glorious as the sun,
    Gratiana steers that noble frame,
Soft as her breast, sweet as her voice
That gave each winding law and poise,
    And swifter than the wings of Fame.

She beat the happy pavement
By such a star made firmament
    Which now no more the roof envies;
But swells up high, with Atlas even,
Bearing the brighter, nobler heaven,
    And, in her, all the deities.

Each step trod out a lover's thought
And the ambitious hopes he brought,
    Chained to her brave feet with such arts,
Such sweet command and gentle awe,
As, when she ceased, we sighing saw
    The floor lay paved with broken hearts.

So did she move; so did she sing,
Like the harmonious spheres that bring
    Unto their rounds their music's aid;

Which she performed such a way
As all the enamoured world will say,
   'The Graces danced, and Apollo played.'

Richard Lovelace (1618-1658)

TO MUSIC, TO BECALM HIS FEVER

Charm me asleep, and melt me so
  With thy delicious numbers,
That being ravished, hence I go
  Away in easy slumbers.
    Ease my sick head,
    And make my bed,
  Thou power that canst sever
    From me this ill;
    And quickly still,
    Though thou not kill
      My fever.

Thou sweetly canst convert the same
  From a consuming fire,
Into a gentle-licking flame,
  And make it thus expire.
  Then make me weep
  My pains asleep,
And give me such reposes,
  That I, poor I,
  May think, thereby,
  I live and die
    'Mongst roses.

Fall on me like a silent dew,
  Or like those maiden showers,

Which, by the peep of day, do strew
　A baptism o'er the flowers.
　　Melt, melt my pains,
　　With my soft strains;
　That having ease me given,
　　With full delight
　　I leave this light,
　　And take my flight
　　　For Heaven.

Robert Herrick (1591-1674)

UPON JULIA'S VOICE

So smooth, so sweet, so silvery is thy voice,
As, could they hear, the damned would make no noise,
But listen to thee, walking in thy chamber,
Melting melodious words to lutes of amber.

Robert Herrick (1591-1674)

TO MUSICK. A SONG

Musick, thou Queen of Heaven, Care-charming-spel,
　That strik'st a stilnesse into hell:
Thou that tam'st Tygers, and fierce storms (that rise)
　With thy soule-melting Lullabies:
Fall down, down, down, from those thy chiming
　spheres,
To charme our soules, as thou enchant'st our eares.

Robert Herrick (1591-1674)

SUPERLATIVE DANCE AND SONG

Shake off your heavy trance,
   And leap into a dance
Such as no mortals use to tread,
   Fit only for Apollo
To play to, for the moon to lead
   And all the stars to follow.

O blessed youths, for Jove doth pause,
Laying aside his graver laws
   For this device;
And at the wedding such a pair
Each dance is taken for a prayer,
   Each song a sacrifice.

Francis Beaumont (1584-1616)

98
In Praise of Music

CHURCH-MUSICK

Sweetest of sweets, I thank you: when displeasure
   Did through my bodie wound my minde,
You took me thence, and in your house of pleasure
   A daintie lodging me assign'd.

Now I in you without a bodie move
   Rising and falling with your wings:
We both together sweetly live and love,
   Yet say sometimes, *God help poore Kings.*

Comfort, I'le die; for if you poste from me,
   Sure I shall do so, and much more:
But if I travell in your companie,
   You know the way to heavens doore.

George Herbert (1593-1633)

TO LUCIA PLAYING ON HER LUTE

When last I heard your nimble fingers play
Upon your lute, nothing so sweet as they
Seemed: all my soul fled ravished to my ear
That sweetly animating sound to hear.
My ravished heart with play kept equal time,
Fell down with you, with you did Ela climb,
Grew sad or lighter, as the tunes you played,
And with your lute a perfect measure made:
If all, so much as I, your music love,
The whole world would at your devotion move;
And at your speaking lute's surpassing charms
Embrace a lasting peace, and fling by arms.

Samuel Pordage (1633-1691?)

Rings on her fingers and bells
   on her toes
And so she makes music wherever
   she goes.

17th Century Nursery Rhyme

   I was all ear
And took in strains that might create a soul
   Under the ribs of death.

John Milton (1608-1674)

THE FAIR SINGER

To make a final conquest of all me,
   Love did compose so sweet an enemy,

In whom both beauties to my death agree,
  Joining themselves in fatal harmony:
That while she with her eyes my heart doth bind,
She with her voice might captivate my mind.

I could have fled from one but singly fair;
  My disentangled soul itself might save,
Breaking the curled trammels of her hair:
  But how should I avoid to be her slave,
Whose subtle art invisibly can wreathe
My fetters of the very air I breathe?

It had been easy fighting in some plain
  Where victory might hang in equal choice;
But all resistance against her is vain,
  Who has the advantage both of eyes and voice:
And all my forces needs must be undone,
She having gained both the wind and sun.

Andrew Marvell (1621-1678)

UPON A RARE VOICE

  When I but hear her sing, I fare
  Like one that, raised, holds his ear
To some bright star in the supremest round;
  Through which, besides the light that's seen,
  There may be heard, from heaven within,
The rest of anthems that the angels sound.

Owen Felltham (1602?-1668)

THE COMMENDATION OF MUSIC

When whispering strains, with creeping wind,
  Distill soft passion through the heart;
And when at every touch we find
  Our pulses beat and bear a part;
    When threads can make
    A heart-string shake,
    Can not deny
  Our souls consist of harmony.

When unto heavenly joys, we feign
  What'er the soul affecteth most,
Which only thus we can explain,
  By music of the heavenly host,
    Whose lays, methinks,
    Make stars to shrink,
    Philosophy
    May judge thereby
  Our souls consist of harmony.

Oh, lull me, lull me, charming air!
  My senses rock with wonder sweet;
Like snow on wool thy fallings are,
  Soft as a spirit's are thy feet;
    Grief who need fear
    That hath an ear?
    Down let him lie
    And slumbering die,
  And change his soul for harmony.

William Strode (1602-1645)

CELIA SINGING

You that think Love can convey
    No other way
But through the eyes, into the heart,
    His fatal dart,
Close up those casements, and but hear
    This siren sing;
    And on the wing
Of her sweet voice, it shall appear
That Love can enter at the ear.

Then unveil your eyes; behold
    The curious mould
Where that voice dwells, and as we know,
    When the cocks crow,
And Sol is mounted on his way,
    We freely may
    Gaze on the day;
So may you, when the music's done,
Awake, and see the rising sun.

Thomas Carew (1595?-1639?)

A SONG FOR ST. CECILIA'S DAY
November 22, 1687

From Harmony, from heav'nly Harmony
    This universal Frame began;
When Nature underneath a heap
    Of jarring Atomes lay,
  And cou'd not heave her Head,
The tuneful Voice was heard from high,
    Arise, ye more than dead.
Then cold and hot and moist and dry,

In order to their Stations leap,
   And MUSICK'S pow'r obey
From Harmony, from heavenly Harmony
   This universal Frame began:
   From Harmony to Harmony
Through all the Compass of the Notes it ran,
The Diapason closing full in Man.

103

The Poet Speaks

2.

What Passion cannot MUSICK raise and quell?
   When *Jubal* struck the corded Shell,
 His listening Brethren stood around,
   And, wond'ring, on their Faces fell
To worship that Celestial Sound:
Less than a God they thought there could not dwell
   Within the hollow of that Shell,
   That spoke so sweetly, and so well.
What Passion cannot MUSICK raise and quell?

3.

The TRUMPET'S loud Clangor
   Excites us to Arms
With shrill Notes of Anger
   And mortal Alarms.
The double double double beat
   Of the thund'ring DRUM
   Cryes, heark the Foes come;
Charge, Charge, 'tis too late to retreat.

4.

   The soft complaining FLUTE
   In dying Notes discovers
   The Woes of hopeless Lovers
Whose Dirge is whisper'd by the warbling LUTE.

5.

    Sharp VIOLINS proclaim
Their jealous Pangs and Desperation,
Fury, frantick Indignation,
Depth of Pains and Heights of Passion
    For the fair, disdainful Dame.

6.

    But oh, what Art can teach
    What human Voice can reach
      The sacred ORGANS Praise?
    Notes inspiring holy Love
Notes that wing their heavenly Ways
    To mend the Choires above.

7.

Orpheus cou'd lead the savage race,
And Trees unrooted left their Place,
    Sequacious of the Lyre;
But bright CECILIA rais'd the Wonder high'r:
When to her Organ vocal Breath was given,
An Angel heard, and straight appear'd
    Mistaking Earth for Heav'n.

GRAND CHORUS

As from the Pow'r of Sacred Lays
    The Spheres began to move,
And sang the great Creator's Praise
    To all the bless'd above;
So, when the last and dreadful Hour
This crumbling Pageant shall devour,
The TRUMPET shall be heard on high,
The dead shall live, and the living die,
And MUSICK shall untune the Sky.

John Dryden (1631-1700)

Music hath charms to soothe the savage breast,
To soften rocks, or bend a knotted oak.

William Congreve (1670-1729) The Morning Bride

There's music in the sighing of the read;
There's music in the gushing of the rill;
There's music in all things, if men had ears.

Lord Byron (1788-1824) Don Juan

FRAGMENT: MUSIC AND SWEET POETRY

How sweet it is to sit and read the tales
  Of mighty poets and to hear the while
Sweet music, which when the attention fails
  Fills the dim pause—

Percy B. Shelley (1792-1822)

A FRAGMENT: TO MUSIC

Silver key of the fountain of tears
  Where the spirit drinks till the brain is wild;
Softest grave of a thousand fears,
  Where their mother, Care, like a drowsy child,
    Is laid asleep in flowers.

Percy B. Shelley (1792-1822)

MUSIC

1.

I pant for the music which is divine,
　My heart in its thirst is a dying flower;
Pour forth the sound like enchanted wine,
　Loosen the notes in a silver shower;
Like a herbless plain, for the gentle rain,
I gasp, I faint, till they wake again.

2.

Let me drink of the spirit of that sweet sound,
　More, oh more,—I am thirsting yet;
It loosens the serpent which care has bound
　Upon my heart to stifle it;
The dissolving strain, through every vein,
　Passes into my heart and brain.

3.

As the scent of a violet withered up,
　Which grew by the brink of a silver lake,
When the hot noon has drained its dewy cup,
　And mist there was none its thirst to slake—
And the violet lay dead while the odour flew
On the wings of the wind o'er the waters blue—

4.

As one who drinks from a charmed cup
　Of foaming, and sparkling, and murmuring wine,
Whom, a mighty Enchantress filling up,
　Invites to love with her kiss divine....

Percy B. Shelley (1792-1822)

THE SINGERS

God sent his singers upon earth
With songs of sadness and of mirth,
That they might touch the hearts of men,
And bring them back to heaven again.

The first a youth, with soul of fire
Held in his hand a golden lyre;
Through groves he wandered, and by streams,
Playing the music of our dreams.

The second, with a bearded face,
Stood singing in the market-place,
And stirred with accents deep and loud
The hearts of all the listening crowd.

A gray, old man, the third and last,
Sang in cathedrals dim and vast
While the majestic organ rolled
Contrition from its mouths of gold.

And those who heard the Singers three
Disputed which the best might be;
For still their music seemed to start
Discordant echoes in each heart.

But the great Master said, "I see
No best in kind, but in degree;
I gave a various gift to each,
To charm, to strengthen, and to teach.

"These are the three great chords of might,
And he whose ear is tuned aright
Will hear no discord in the three,
But the most perfect harmony."

Henry Wadsworth Longfellow (1807-1882)

Who hears music, feels his solitude
Peopled at once.

Robert Browning (1812-1889) Balaustion's Adventure

MUSIC

On music drawn away, a sea-borne mariner
   Star over bowsprit pale,
Beneath a roof of mist or depths of lucid air
   I put out under sail;

Breastbone my steady bow and lungs full, running free
   Before a following gale,
I ride the rolling back and mass of every sea
   By Night wrapt in her veil;

All passions and all joys that vessels undergo
   Tremble alike in me;
Fair wind or waves in havoc when the trumpets blow

   On the enormous sea
Rock me, and level calms come silvering sea and air
   A glass for my despair.

Charles Baudelaire (1821-67) Translated by Robert Fitzgerald

We, in fact, have made writing a definite mode of composition, and have treated it as a form of elaborate design. The Greeks, upon the other hand, regarded writing simply as a method of chronicling. Their test was always the spoken word in its musical and metrical relations. The voice was the medium, and the ear was the critic. I have sometimes thought the story of Homer's blindness might be really an artistic myth, created in critical days, and serving to remind us, not merely that the great poet is always a seer, seeing less with the eyes of the body than he does with the eyes of the soul, but that he is a true singer also, building his song out of music, repeating each line over and over again to himself till he has caught the secret of its melody, chaunting in darkness the words that are winged with light.

Oscar Wilde (1854-1900) The Critic as Artist

109
The Poet Speaks

. . . It is at once by poetry and *through* poetry, by music and *through* music, that the soul divines what splendors shine behind the tomb . . .

Edgar Allan Poe (1809-1849) The Poetic Principle

. . . And thus when by Poetry—or when by Music, the most entrancing of the Poetic moods—we find ourselves melted into tears—not as the Abbaté Gravia supposes—through excess of pleasure, but through a certain petulant, impatient sorrow at our inability to grasp *now* wholly, here on earth, at once and forever, those divine and rapturous joys, of which *through* the poem, or *through* the music, we attain to but brief and indeterminate glimpses.

The struggle to apprehend the supernal Loveliness—this struggle, on the part of souls fittingly constituted—has given to the world all *that* which it (the world) has ever been enabled at once to understand and *to feel* as poetic.

The Poetic Sentiment, of course, may develop itself in various modes—in Painting, in Sculpture, in Architecture, in the Dance—very especially in Music,—and very peculiarly, and with a wide field, in the composition of the Landscape Garden. Our present theme, however, has regard only to its manifestation in words. And here let me speak briefly on the topic of rhythm. Contenting myself with the certainty that Music, in its various modes of metre, rhythm, and rhyme, is of so vast a moment in Poetry as never to be wisely rejected—is so vitally important an adjunct, that he is simply silly who declines its assistance, I will not now pause to maintain its absolute essentiality. It is in Music, perhaps, that the soul most nearly attains the great end for which, when inspired by the Poetic Sentiment, it struggles—the creation of supernal Beauty. It *may* be, indeed, that here this sublime end is, now and then, attained *in fact*. We are often made to feel, with a shivering delight, that from an earthly harp are striken notes which *cannot* have been unfamiliar to the angels. And thus there can be little doubt that in the union of Poetry with Music in its popular sense, we shall find the widest field for Poetic development. The old Bards and Minnesingers had advantages which we do not possess—and Thomas Moore, singing his own songs, was, in the most legitimate manner, perfecting them as poems.

Edgar Allan Poe (1809-1849) The Poetic Principle

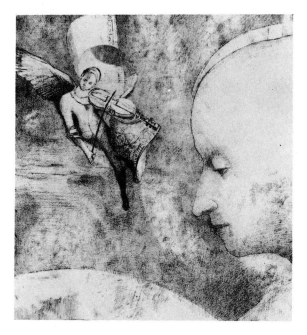

.... and there is, I am persuaded, a world of profound mathematics in this matter of music; indeed no one can doubt that.

Gerard M. Hopkins (1844-1889) Letter to R. W. Dixon

All keys are the same to me and to every one who thinks that music was before instruments and angels before tortoises and cats.

Gerard M. Hopkins (1844-1889) Letter to Robert Bridges

THAT MUSIC ALWAYS ROUND ME

That music always round me, unceasing, unbeginning, yet long untaught
   I did not hear,
But now the chorus I hear and am elated,
A tenor, strong, ascending with power and health, with glad notes of day-
   break I hear,
A soprano at intervals sailing buoyantly over the tops of immense waves,
A transparent base shuddering lusciously under and through the universe,
The triumphant tutti, the funeral wailings with sweet flutes and violins, all
   these I fill myself with,
I hear not the volumes of sound merely, I am moved by the exquisite mean-
   ings,
I listen to the different voices winding in and out, striving, contending with
   fiery vehemence to excel each other in emotion;
I do not think the performers know themselves—but now I think I begin
   to know them.

Walt Whitman (1819-1892)

THE ART OF POETRY

Music must be paramount:
Choose for this an Uneven Rhythm,
More indefinite, more soluble in air,
With nothing to press or bind.

You must not hesitate to choose
Your words with some ambiguity:
The best song is a hazy song
Where Vagueness and Precision join.

There, are eyes beautiful and veiled,
And the quivering light of high noon,
There, in a cooled autumnal sky,
Is a blue confusion of bright stars.

For we must have Nuance still,
Not Color-nothing but nuance!
Ah! only nuance can betroth
Dream to dream and flute to horn!

Flee far as possible from deadly Jest,
From cruel Wit and impure Laughter,
That make the eyes of Heaven weep—
Avoid this garlic of low-class kitchens!

Take eloquence and wring its neck!
And while you are in the mood, try
To moderate Rhyme a little more.
If you don't, what limit will it reach?

Who can tell the wrongs that Rhyme has done?
What deaf child or crazy Negro
Fashioned us this bauble from a coin
That rings false and hollow under the file?

Music, always more music!
Let your verse be the winged thing
We feel soaring from a soul on its way
To other loves in other heavens.

Let your verse be a good-luck charm
Scattered on the brisk morning wind
That passes smelling of mint and thyme . . . .
And everything else is mere literature.

Paul Verlaine (1844-1896) Translated by Muriel Kittel

113
The Poet Speaks

Happy musician! The evolution of his art has given him a privileged position. His means are well defined, the substance of his composition lies elaborated before him. One can compare him to the bee when she is concerned only with her honey. The regular combs and waxen cells are all laid out before her. Her task is well gauged and restricted to the best of herself. Such is the composer. One might say the music pre-exists and awaits him. It has been formed for a long time!

Paul Valéry (1871-1945) Remarks on Poetry

To Paul Valéry, May 5, 1891

In order to give life and meaning to literature, we must reach that "great symphony." Perhaps no one ever will. Nevertheless, the ideal has obsessed even the most unconscious writers, and its main lines—however gross or fine—are to be found in every written work. The perfect poem we dream of can be suggested by Music itself; and if our own written melody seems imperfect when it has ceased, we must lay siege to the other and plagiarize.

Stéphane Mallarmé (1842-98)

THE FIDDLER OF DOONEY

When I play on my fiddle in Dooney,
Folk dance like a wave of the sea;
My cousin is priest in Kilvarnet,
My brother in Mocharabuiee.

I passed my brother and cousin:
They read in their books of prayer;
I read in my books of songs
I bought at the Sligo fair.

When we come at the end of time
To Peter sitting in state,
He will smile on the three old spirits,
But call me first through the gate;

For the good are always the merry,
Save by an evil chance,
And the merry love the fiddle,
And the merry love to dance:

And when the folk there spy me,
They will all come up to me,
With 'Here is the fiddler of Dooney!'
And dance like a wave of the sea.

William Butler Yeats (1865-1939)

THE PLAYERS ASK FOR A BLESSING ON THE PSALTERIES AND ON THEMSELVES

Three Voices (together). Hurry to bless the hands that play,
 The mouths that speak, the notes and strings,
 O masters of the glittering town!
 O! lay the shrilly trumpet down,
 Though drunken with the flags that sway
 Over the ramparts and the towers,
 And with the waving of your wings.

First Voice. Maybe they linger by the way.
   One gathers up his purple gown;
   One leans and mutters by the wall—
   He dreads the weight of mortal hours.

Second Voice. O no, O no! they hurry down
   Like plovers that have heard the call.

Third Voice. O kinsmen of the Three in One,
   O kinsmen, bless the hands that play.
   The notes they waken shall live on
   When all this heavy history's done;
   Our hands, our hands must ebb away.

Three Voices (together). The proud and careless notes live on,
   But bless our hands that ebb away.

William Butler Yeats (1865-1939)

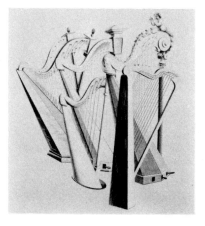

THE PAVILION OF MUSIC

The musicians have gone.
The lilacs which they placed
   in the vases of jade
   bend toward the lutes
   and seem to listen still.

Chang-Wou-Kien (1879-)

Music rots when it gets too far from the dance. Poetry atrophies when it gets too far from music.

Ezra Pound (1885-) The ABC of Reading

Poetry is a composition of words set to music. Most other definitions of it are indefensible, or metaphysical. The proportion or quality of the music may, and does, vary; but poetry withers and 'dries out' when it leaves music, or at least an imagined music, too far behind it. The horrors of modern 'readings of poetry' are due to oratorical recitation. Poetry must be read as music and not as oratory. I do not mean that the words should be jumbled together and made indistinct and unrecognizable in a sort of onomatopoeic paste. I have found few save musicians who pay the least attention to the poet's own music. They are often, I admit, uncritical of his verbal excellence or deficit, ignorant of his 'literary' value or bathos. But the literary qualities are not the whole of our art.

Poets who are not interested in music are, or become, bad poets. I would almost say that poets should never be too long out of touch with musicians. Poets who will not study music are defective. I do not mean that they need become virtuosi, or that they need necessarily undergo the musical curriculum of their time. It is perhaps their value that they can be a little refractory and heretical, for all arts tend to decline into the stereotype; and at all times the mediocre tend or try, semi-consciously or unconsciously, to obscure the fact that the day's fashion is not the immutable.

Music and poetry, melody and versification, alike fall under the marasmus.

It is too late to prevent vers libre. But, conceivably, one might improve it, and one might stop at least a little of the idiotic and narrow discussion on an ignorance of music. Bigoted attack, born of this ignorance of the tradition of music, was what we had to live through.

Ezra Pound (1885-   ) Vers Libre and Arnold Dolmetsch

MUSIC

I have been urged by earnest violins
And drunk their mellow sorrows to the slake
Of all my sorrows and my thirsting sins.
My heart has beaten for a brave drum's sake.

Huge chords have wrought me mighty: I have hurled
Thuds of God's thunder. And with old winds pondered
Over the curse of this chaotic world,
With low lost winds that maundered as they wandered.

I have been gay with trivial fifes that laugh;
And songs more sweet than possible things are sweet;
And gongs, and oboes. Yet I guessed not half
Life's sympathy till I had made hearts beat,
And touched Love's body into trembling cries,
And blown my love's lips into laughs and sighs.

Wilfred Owen (1893-1918)

Strings in the earth and air
    Make music sweet;
Strings by the river where
    The willows meet.

There's music along the river
    For Love wanders there,
Pale flowers on his mantle,
    Dark leaves on his hair.

All softly playing
    With head to the music bent
And fingers straying
    Upon an instrument.

James Joyce (1882-1941) Chamber Music

Listen, my heart, in his flute is the music of the smell of wild flowers, of the glistening leaves and gleaming water, of shadows resonant with bee's wings.

The flute steals his smile from my friend's lips and spreads it over my life.

Rabindranath Tagore (1861-1941) Fruit-Gathering

ON HEARING A SYMPHONY OF BEETHOVEN

Sweet sounds, oh, beautiful music, do not cease!
Reject me not into the world again.
With you alone is excellence and peace,
Mankind made plausible, his purpose plain.
Enchanted in your air benign and shrewd,
With limbs a-sprawl and empty faces pale,
The spiteful and the stingy and the rude
Sleep like the scullions in the fairy-tale.
This moment is the best the world can give:
The tranquil blossom on the tortured stem.
Reject me not, sweet sounds! oh, let me live,
Till Doom espy my towers and scatter them,
A city spell-bound under the aging sun,
Music my rampart, and my only one.

Edna St. Vincent Millay (1892-1950)

I think that a poet may gain much from the study of music: how much technical knowledge of musical form is desirable I do not know for I have not that technical knowledge myself. But I believe that the properties in which music concerns the poet most nearly, are the sense of rhythm and the sense of structure. I think that it might be possible for a poet to work too closely to musical analogies: the result might be an effect of artificiality; but I know that a poem, or a passage of a poem, may tend to realize itself first as a particular rhythm before it reaches expression in words, and that this rhythm may bring to birth the idea and the image; and I do not believe that this is an experience peculiar to myself. The use of recurrent themes is as natural to poetry as to music. There are possibilities for verse which bear some analogy to the development of a theme by different groups of instruments; there are possibilities of transitions in a poem comparable to the different movements of a symphony or a quartet; there are possibilties of contrapuntal arrangement of subject-matter. It is in the concert room, rather than in the opera house, that the germ of a poem may be quickened. More than this I cannot say, but must leave the matter here to those who have had a musical education.

T. S. Eliot (1888-   ) The Music of Poetry

THE DANCE

In Breughel's great picture, The Kermess,
the dancers go round, they go round and
around, the squeal and the blare and the
tweedle of bagpipes, a bugle and fiddles
tipping their bellies (round as the thick-
sided glasses whose wash they impound)
their hips and their bellies off balance
to turn them. Kicking and rolling about
the Fair-Grounds, swinging their butts, those
shanks must be sound to bear up under such
rollicking measures, prance as they dance
in Breughel's great picture, The Kermess.

William Carlos Williams (1883-   )

I used to practice writing poetry as a pianist practices. I would take a waltz or a polka, some gay music-hall song or perhaps the song of the barrel organ beneath my window and translate it into words.

Edith Sitwell (1887-   )

Inspiration and song are the irreducible final qualities of a poet which make the vocation different from all others. Inspiration is an experience in which a line or an idea is given to one, and perhaps also a state of mind in which one writes one's best poetry. Song is far more difficult to define. It is the music which a poem as yet unthought of will assume, the empty womb of poetry for ever in the poet's consciousness, waiting for the fertilizing seed.

Sometimes, when I lie in a state of half-waking half-sleeping, I am conscious of a stream of words which seem to pass through my mind, without their having a meaning, but they have a sound, a sound of passion, or a sound recalling poetry that I know. Again sometimes when I am writing, the music of the words I am trying to shape takes me far beyond the words, I am aware of a rhythm, a dance, a fury, which is as yet empty of words.

Stephen Spender (1909-   ) The Making of a Poem

THE COMPOSER

All the others translate; the painter sketches
A visible world to love or reject;
Rummaging into his living, the poet fetches
The images out that hurt and connect.

From Life to Art by painstaking adaption,
Relying on us to cover the rift;
Only your notes are pure contraption,
Only your song is an absolute gift.

Pour out your presence, O delight, cascading
The falls of the knee and the weirs of the spine,
Our climate of silence and doubt invading;

You alone, alone, O imaginary song,
Are unable to say an existence is wrong,
And pour out your forgiveness like a wine.

W. H. Auden (1907-   )

MUSICIAN

Where have these hands been,
By what delayed,
That so long stayed
Apart from the thin

Strings which they now grace
With their lonely skill
Music and their cool will
At last interlace.

Now with great ease, and slow,
The thumb, the finger, the strong
Delicate hand plucks the long
String it was born to know.

And, under the palm, the string
Sings as it wished to sing.

Louise Bogan (1897-   )

Just as my fingers on these keys
Make music, so the selfsame sounds
On my spirit make a music too.

Music is feeling, then, not sound;
And thus it is that what I feel
Here in this room, desiring you,

Thinking of your blue-shadowed silk
Is music.

Wallace Stevens (1879-1955) Peter Quince at the Clavier

MUSIC

When music sounds, gone is the earth I know,
And all her lovely things even lovelier grow;
Her flowers in vision flame, her forest trees
Lift burdened branches, stilled with ecstasies.

When music sounds, out of the water rise
Naiads whose beauty dims my waking eyes,
Rapt in strange dreams burns each enchanted face,
With solemn echoing stirs their dwelling-place.

When music sounds, all that I was I am
Ere to this haunt of brooding dust I came;
While from Time's woods break into distant song
The swift-winged hours, as I hasten along.

Walter De La Mare (1873-1956)

Credits

Thanks are due to the following museums for allowing material from their collections to be reproduced in this anthology: